Early Praise for *Web Development with Clojure*

This is a great resource and one I will insist all my trainee Clojure web developers read.

➤ Colin Yates, principal engineer and technical team leader, QFI Consulting LLP

Clojure is an awesome language, and using it for developing web applications is pure joy. This book is a valuable and timely resource for getting started with the various libraries of the Clojure web-development toolbox.

➤ Fred Daoud, web-development specialist and coauthor of *Seven Web Frameworks in Seven Weeks*

In *Web Development with Clojure*, Dmitri Sotnikov manages to take the sting out of getting started building real applications with Clojure. If you know the basics but are still trying to "get" Clojure, this is the book for you.

➤ Russ Olsen, vice president, consulting services, Cognitect

Sotnikov illustrates Clojure's flexible approach to web development by teaching the use of state-of-the-art libraries in making realistic websites.

➤ Chris Houser, *Joy of Clojure* coauthor

With this book, you'll jump right into web development using powerful functional programming techniques. As you follow along, you'll make your app more scalable and maintainable—and you'll bring the expressiveness of Clojure to your client-side JavaScript.

➤ Ian Dees, author, *Cucumber Recipes*

Dmitri's book successfully walks a narrow line of introducing language features while also solving real, modern software-development problems. This represents a significant return on investment for the time you devote to a technical book.

➤ **Brian Sletten, Bosatsu Consulting, author of *Resource-Oriented Architecture Patterns for Webs of Data***

This is a fast-paced, no-cruft intro to applying your Clojure chops to making web apps. From Chapter 1 you're running a real web app and then adding databases, security, JavaScript, and more. No dogma, no preaching, no fluff! To the point, productive, and clear. This book gives you all you need to get started and have a real app that you can continue to grow.

➤ **Sam Griffith Jr., polyglot programmer at Interactive Web Systems, LLC**

Web Development with Clojure

Build Bulletproof Web Apps with Less Code

Dmitri Sotnikov

The Pragmatic Bookshelf

Dallas, Texas • Raleigh, North Carolina

Pragmatic Bookshelf

Many of the designations used by manufacturers and sellers to distinguish their products are claimed as trademarks. Where those designations appear in this book, and The Pragmatic Programmers, LLC was aware of a trademark claim, the designations have been printed in initial capital letters or in all capitals. The Pragmatic Starter Kit, The Pragmatic Programmer, Pragmatic Programming, Pragmatic Bookshelf, PragProg and the linking *g* device are trademarks of The Pragmatic Programmers, LLC.

Every precaution was taken in the preparation of this book. However, the publisher assumes no responsibility for errors or omissions, or for damages that may result from the use of information (including program listings) contained herein.

Our Pragmatic courses, workshops, and other products can help you and your team create better software and have more fun. For more information, as well as the latest Pragmatic titles, please visit us at *http://pragprog.com*.

The team that produced this book includes:

Michael Swaine (editor)
Potomac Indexing, LLC (indexer)
Candace Cunningham (copyeditor)
David J Kelly (typesetter)
Janet Furlow (producer)
Juliet Benda (rights)
Ellie Callahan (support)

Printed in the United States of America.
ISBN-13: 978-1-937785-64-2
Printed on acid-free paper.
Book version: P1.0—January 2014

Contents

Introduction

This book's cover has a bonsai tree on it. I chose it to represent elegance and simplicity, as these qualities make Clojure such an attractive language. A good software project is like a bonsai. You have to meticulously craft it to take the shape you want, and the tool you use should make it a pleasant experience. I hope to convince you here that Clojure is that tool.

What You Need

This book is aimed at readers of all levels. While having some basic proficiency with functional programming will be helpful, it's by no means required to follow the material in this book. If you're not a Clojure user already, this book is a good starting point, as it focuses on applying the language to solve concrete problems. This means we'll focus on a small number of language features needed to build common web applications.

Why Clojure?

Clojure is a small language that has simplicity and correctness as its primary goals. Being a functional language, it emphasizes immutability and declarative programming. As you'll see in this book, these features make it easy and idiomatic to write clean and correct code.

There are many languages to choose from and as many opinions on what makes any one of them a good language. Some languages are simple but verbose. You've probably heard people say that verbosity really doesn't matter, the argument being that when two languages are Turing complete, anything that can be written in one language can also be written in the other with a bit of extra code.

I think that's missing the point, however. The real question is not whether something can be expressed in principle. It's how well the language maps to the problem being solved. One language will let you think in terms of your problem domain while another will force you to translate the problem to its constructs.

The latter is often tedious and rarely enjoyable. You end up writing a lot of boilerplate code and constantly repeating yourself. There's a certain amount of irony involved in having to write repetitive code.

Other languages aren't verbose and they provide many different tools for solving problems. Unfortunately, having many tools does not directly translate into higher productivity.

The more features there are, the more things you have to keep in your head to work with the language effectively. With many languages I find myself constantly expending mental overhead thinking about all the different features and how they interact with one another.

What matters to me in a language is whether I can use it without thinking about it. When a language is lacking in expressiveness I'm acutely aware that I'm writing code that I shouldn't be. On the other hand, when a language has too many features I often feel overwhelmed or I get distracted playing with them.

To make an analogy with mathematics, having a general formula that you can derive others from is better than having to memorize a whole bunch of formulas for specific problems.

This is where Clojure comes in. It allows us to easily derive a solution to a particular problem from a small set of general patterns. All you need to become productive is to learn a few simple concepts and a bit of syntax. These concepts can then be combined in a myriad ways to solve all kinds of problems.

Why Make Web Apps in Clojure?

Clojure boasts tens of thousands of users; it's used in a wide range of settings, including banks and hospitals. Clojure is likely the most popular Lisp dialect today for starting new development. Despite being a young language, it has proven itself in serious production systems and the feedback from users has been overwhelmingly positive.

As web development is one of the major domains for using Clojure, several popular libraries and frameworks have sprouted in this area. The Clojure web stack is based on the Ring and Compojure libraries.[1,2] Ring is the base HTTP library, while Compojure provides routing on top of it. In the following chapters you'll become familiar with the web stack and how to use it effectively to build your web applications.

---

1.   https://github.com/ring-clojure/ring
2.   https://github.com/weavejester/compojure

There are many platforms for doing web development, so why should you choose Clojure over other options?

Well, consider those options. Many popular platforms force you to make trade-offs. Some platforms lack performance, others require a lot of boilerplate, and others lack the infrastructure necessary for real-world applications.

Clojure addresses the questions of performance and infrastructure by being a hosted language. The Java Virtual Machine is a mature and highly performant environment with great tooling and deployment options. Clojure brings expressive power akin to that of Ruby and Python to this excellent platform. When working with Clojure you won't have to worry about being limited by your runtime when your application grows.

The most common way to handle the boilerplate in web applications is by using a framework. There are many frameworks, such as Ruby on Rails, Django, and Spring. The frameworks provide canned functionality needed for building a modern site.

The benefits the frameworks offer also come with inherent costs. Since many operations are done implicitly, you have to memorize what effects any action might have. This opaqueness makes your code more difficult to reason about. When you need to do something that is at odds with the framework's design it can quickly become awkward and difficult. You might have to dive deep into the internals of the particular framework and create hacks around the expected behaviors.

So instead of using frameworks, Clojure makes a number of powerful libraries available, and we can put these libraries together in a way that makes sense for our particular project. As you'll see, we manage to avoid having to write boilerplate while retaining the code clarity we desire. As you read on I think you'll agree that this model has clear advantages over the framework-based approach.

My goal is to give you both a solid understanding of the Clojure web stack and the expertise to quickly and easily build web applications using it. The following chapters will guide you all the way from setting up your development environment to having a complete real-world application. I will show what's available, then guide you in structuring your application using the current best practices.

CHAPTER 1

Getting Your Feet Wet

In the *Introduction*, on page ix, we talked about some of the benefits of the functional style when it comes to writing applications. Of course, you can't learn a language simply by reading about it. To really get a feel for it you have to write some code yourself.

In this chapter we'll cover how to develop a simple guestbook application that allows users to leave messages for each other. We'll see the basic structure of a web application as well as the tools necessary for effective Clojure development. If you're new to Clojure, I recommend taking a look at Appendix 2, *Clojure Primer*, on page 181, for a crash course on the basic concepts and syntax.

Setting Up Your Environment

Clojure requires the Java Virtual Machine (JVM) to run, and you will need a working Java Development Kit, version 1.6 or higher.[1] Clojure distribution is provided as a JAR that simply needs to be available on your project's classpath. Clojure applications can be built with the standard Java tools, such as Maven and Ant;[2,3] however, I strongly recommend that you use Leiningen,[4] which is designed specifically for Clojure.

Managing Projects with Leiningen

Leiningen lets you create, build, test, package, and deploy your projects. In other words, it's your one-stop shop for all your project-management-related needs.

---

1. http://www.oracle.com/technetwork/java/javase/downloads/index.html
2. http://maven.apache.org/
3. http://ant.apache.org/
4. http://leiningen.org/

Leiningen is the Clojure counterpart of Maven, a popular tool for managing Java dependencies. Leiningen is compatible with Maven, so it has access to large and well-maintained repositories of Java libraries. In addition, Clojure libraries are commonly found in the Clojars repository.[5] This repository is, of course, enabled by default in Leiningen.

With Leiningen, you don't need to worry about manually downloading all the libraries for your project. You can simply specify the top-level dependencies, and they will cause the libraries they depend on to be pulled in automatically.

Installing Leiningen is as simple as downloading the installation script from the official project page and running it.[6]

Let's test this. We'll create a new project by downloading the script and running the following commands:

```
wget https://raw.github.com/technomancy/leiningen/stable/bin/lein
chmod +x lein
mv lein ~/bin
lein new myapp
```

Since we're running lein for the first time, it will need to install itself. Once the install is finished you should see the following output if the command completes successfully:

```
Generating a project called myapp based on the 'default' template.
To see other templates (app, lein plug-in, etc), try `lein help new`.
```

A new folder called myapp has been created, containing a skeleton application. The code for the application can be found in the src folder. There we'll have another folder called myapp containing a single source file named core.clj. This file has the following code inside:

```
(ns myapp.core)

(defn foo
  "I don't do a whole lot."
  [x]
  (println x "Hello, World!"))
```

Note that the namespace declaration matches the folder structure. Since the core namespace is inside the myapp folder, its name is myapp.core.

---

5.   https://clojars.org/
6.   http://leiningen.org/#install

What's in the Leiningen Project File

Inside the myapp project folder we have a project.clj file. This file contains the description of our application. With close scrutiny, you'll see that this file is written using standard Clojure syntax and contains the application name, version, URL, license, and dependencies.

```
(defproject myapp "0.1.0-SNAPSHOT"
  :description "FIXME: write description"
  :url "http://example.com/FIXME"
  :license {:name "Eclipse Public License"
            :url "http://www.eclipse.org/legal/epl-v10.html"}
  :dependencies [[org.clojure/clojure "1.5.1"]])
```

The project.clj file will allow us to manage many different aspects of our application, as well. For example, we could set the foo function from the myapp.core namespace as the entry point for the application using the :main key:

```
(defproject myapp "0.1.0-SNAPSHOT"
  :description "FIXME: write description"
  :url "http://example.com/FIXME"
  :license {:name "Eclipse Public License"
            :url "http://www.eclipse.org/legal/epl-v10.html"}
  :dependencies [[org.clojure/clojure "1.5.1"]]
  ;;this will set foo as the main function
  :main myapp.core/foo)
```

The application can now be run from the command line using lein run. Since the foo function expects an argument, we'll have to pass one in:

```
lein run First
First Hello, World!
```

In the preceding example we created a very simple application that has only a single dependency: the Clojure runtime. If we used this as the base for a web application, then we'd have to write a lot of boilerplate to get it up and running. Let's see how we can use a Leiningen template to create a web-application project with all the boilerplate already set up.

Leiningen Templates

The templates consist of skeleton projects that are instantiated when the name of the template is supplied to the lein script. The templates themselves are simply Clojure projects that use the lein-newnew plug-in.[7] Later on we'll see how we can create such templates ourselves.

---

7.   https://github.com/Raynes/lein-newnew

For now, we'll use the *compojure-app* template to instantiate our next applica-tion.[8] The template name is specified as the argument following the new keyword when running lein, followed by the name of the project. To make a web application instead of the default one as we did a moment ago, we only have to do the following:

```
lein new compojure-app guestbook
```

This will cause Leiningen to use the *compojure-app* template when creating the guestbook application. This type of application needs to start up a web server in order to run. To do that we can run lein ring server instead of lein run.

When we run the application, we'll see the following output in the console and a new browser window will pop up showing the home page.

```
lein ring server
guestbook is starting
2013-07-14 18:21:06.603:INFO:oejs.Server:jetty-7.6.1.v20120215
2013-07-14 18:21:06.639:INFO:oejs.AbstractConnector:
StartedSelectChannelConnector@0.0.0.0:3000
Started server on port 3000
```

Now that we know how to create and run our applications, we'll look at our editor options.

You might have noticed that Clojure code can quickly end up having lots of parentheses. Keeping them balanced by hand would quickly turn into an exercise in frustration. Luckily, Clojure editors will do this for us.

In fact, not only do the editors balance the parentheses, but some are even structurally aware. This means the editor knows where one expression ends and another begins. Therefore, we can navigate and select code in terms of blocks of logic instead of lines of text.

In this chapter we'll be using Light Table to work with our guestbook applica-tion.[9] It's very easy to get up and running and will allow us to quickly dive into writing some code. However, its functionality is somewhat limited and you may find it insufficient for larger projects. Alternative development envi-ronments are discussed in Appendix 1, *Alternative IDE Options*, on page 177.

Using Light Table

Light Table does not require any installation and we can simply run the exe-cutable after it's downloaded.

---

8. https://github.com/yogthos/compojure-template
9. http://www.lighttable.com/

Light Table offers a very minimal look. By default it simply shows the editor pane with the welcome message (see the following figure).

Figure 1—Light Table workspace

We'll add the *workspace* pane from the menu by selecting *View -> Workspace* or pressing Ctrl-T on Windows/Linux or Cmd-T on OS X.

From there we can open the guestbook project by navigating to the Folder tab on the top left, as the following figure shows.

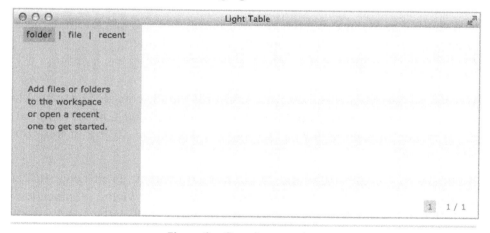

Figure 2—Opening a project

Once the project is selected we can navigate the project tree and select files we wish to edit (see the following figure).

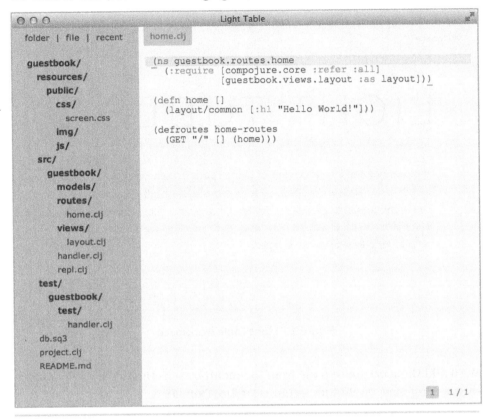

Figure 3—Light Table project

Now that we have our development environment set up, we can finally look at adding some functionality to our guestbook application.

Your First Project

You should have your guestbook project running in the console and available at http://localhost:3000/. We'll stop this instance by pressing Ctrl-C in the terminal. Since we have it open in our Light Table workspace, we can run it from the editor instead.

We'll now go a step further and create a Read-Evaluate-Print Loop (REPL) connection from Light Table to our project. Navigate to *View -> Connections* in the menu to open the Connections tab. There we can click the Add Connection button shown in Figure 4, *Light Table connection*, on page 7.

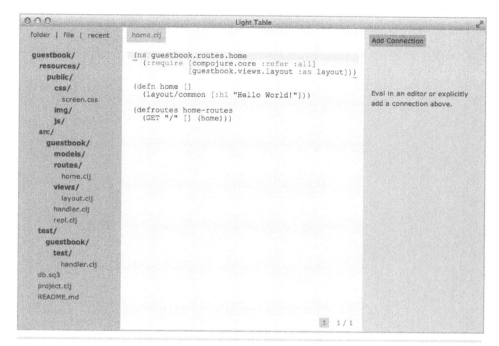

Figure 4—Light Table connection

At this point a list of different connection options will pop up. We'll select the *Clojure* option, as seen in Figure 5, *Light Table Clojure connection*, on page 8. Then we'll navigate to the guestbook project folder and select the project.clj file.

With our project connected to Light Table we can start evaluating things right in the editor!

You can try this immediately by navigating to any function and pressing Ctrl-Enter on Windows and Linux or Cmd-Enter on OS X. If we do this while the cursor is on the home function, we'll see the following printed next to it:

```
#'guestbook.routes.home/home
```

This says that the function has been evaluated in the REPL and is now available for use.

We can also open an Instarepl by pressing Ctrl+spacebar and typing in *repl*. This will open a scratch editor that we can use to run arbitrary code (see Figure 6, *Light Table Instarepl*, on page 8).

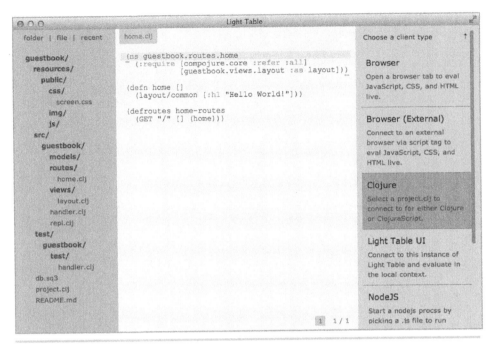

Figure 5—Light Table Clojure connection

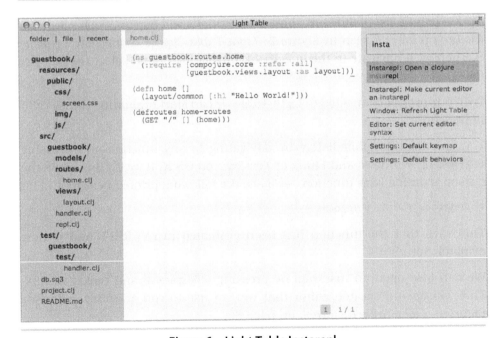

Figure 6—Light Table Instarepl

By default the Instarepl evaluates everything as soon as any changes are made. This is referred to as the *live* mode. We can now reference the guest-book.repl namespace here and run the start-server function.

```
(use 'guestbook.repl)
(start-server)
```

When the code is evaluated the HTTP server will start up and a new browser window will open, pointing to the home page (as in the following figure).

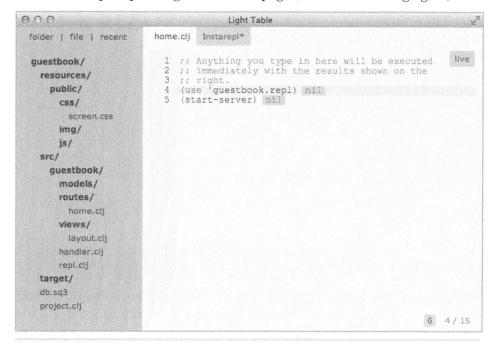

Figure 7—Running the server in the Instarepl

Since we don't wish start-server to continue being called, we'll remove the preceding code from the editor.

Alternatively, we could disable the live evaluation by clicking the *live* icon on the top right. With the live mode disabled we can run commands using Alt-Enter.

Now let's reference our home namespace by running (use 'guestbook.routes.home) and call the home function, as Figure 8, *Using the REPL*, on page 10 shows.

As you can see, calling home simply generates an HTML string for our home page. This is what gets rendered in the browser when we navigate to http://localhost:3000.

Figure 8—Using the REPL

Notice that we use Clojure vectors to represent the corresponding HTML tags in our code. If we add some new tags and reload the page, we'll see the changes. For example, let's update our home function to display a heading and a form to enter a message.

```
(defn home []
  (layout/common
    [:h1 "Guestbook"]
    [:p "Welcome to my guestbook"]
    [:hr]
    [:form
     [:p "Name:"]
     [:input]
     [:p "Message:"]
     [:textarea {:rows 10 :cols 40}]]))
```

When we reload the page, we'll immediately see the changes we made (refer to Figure 9, *Guestbook*, on page 11).

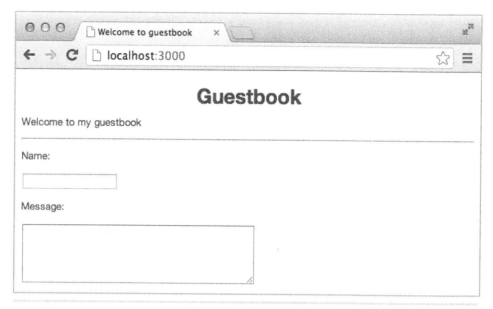

Figure 9—Guestbook

You might have guessed that the code directly below the home function is responsible for binding the "/" route to it.

```
(defroutes home-routes
  (GET "/" [] (home)))
```

Here, we use defroutes to define the routes for the guestbook.routes.home namespace. Each route represents a URI to which your application responds. It starts with the type of the HTTP request it responds to, such as GET or POST, followed by the parameters and the body.

Before we move on to add any more functionality to the project, we'll take a quick look at the files that were generated for our guestbook application.

Understanding Application Structure

When we expand our project in the *Workspace* tab it should look like this:

```
guestbook/
  resources/
    public/
      css/
        screen.css
      img/
      js/
  src
    guestbook/
```

```
    models/
    routes/
      home.clj
    views/
      layout.clj
    handler.clj
    repl.clj
  test/
    guestbook/
      test/
        hanlder.clj
  project.clj
  README.md
```

In our project's root folder is the project.clj file that is used for configuring and building the application.

We also have several folders in our project. The src folder is where the application code lives. The resources folder is where we'll put any static resources associated with the application, such as CSS files, images, and JavaScript. Finally, we have the test folder where we can add tests for our application.

Clojure namespaces follow Java packaging conventions, meaning that if a namespace contains a prefix, it must live in a folder matching the name of the prefix. Note that if a namespace contains any dashes, they must be converted to underscores for the corresponding folder and file names.

This is because the dash is not a valid character in Java package names. Given that Clojure compiles to JVM bytecode, it must follow this convention as well.

Since we called our application guestbook, all its namespaces live under the src/guestbook folder. Let's look at what these are. First we have the guestbook.handler namespace found in src/guestbook/handler.clj. This namespace contains the entry point to our application and defines the handler that's going to handle all the requests to it.

The guestbook.repl namespace found in src/guestbook/repl.clj contains functions that start and stop the server when running from the REPL. We can use it to launch our application directly from the editor instead of running it via lein.

Next, we have a folder called models. This is reserved for namespaces used to define the application's model layer. Such namespaces might deal with database connections, table definitions, and records access.

In the routes folder we have the namespaces dealing with the route definitions. The routes constitute entry points for any workflows we choose to implement.

Currently, there's a single namespace called guestbook.routes.home with the route to your home page defined in it. This namespace lives in src/guestbook/routes/home.clj.

The views folder comes next; it's used to hold namespaces that deal with your application's visual layout. It comes populated with the guestbook.views.layout namespace, which defines the basic page structure. Once again, the corresponding file for the layout namespace is src/guestbook/views/layout.clj.

Adding Some Functionality

Let's look at creating the user interface (UI) for our guestbook. Don't worry if you can't immediately follow all of the code; it will be covered in detail in the following chapters. Instead of focusing on the minutiae of each function, notice how we'll structure our application and where we put different parts of application logic.

We created a form earlier by writing out its tags by hand. We'll now replace it with a better implementation using helper functions from the Hiccup library.[10]

In order to use these functions, we'll have to reference the library in our namespace declaration as seen here:

```
(ns guestbook.routes.home
  (:require [compojure.core :refer :all]
            [guestbook.views.layout :as layout]
            [hiccup.form :refer :all]))
```

We'll start by creating a function to render the existing messages. This function renders an HTML list containing the existing comments. For the time being we'll simply hardcode a couple of test comments.

```
(defn show-guests []
 [:ul.guests
   (for [{:keys [message name timestamp]}
        [{:message "Howdy" :name "Bob" :timestamp nil}
         {:message "Hello" :name "Bob" :timestamp nil}]]
    [:li
      [:blockquote message]
      [:p "-" [:cite name]]
      [:time timestamp]])])
```

Next, let's update the home function to allow the guests to see the messages left by the previous guests, and provide a form to create a new message.

---

10. https://github.com/weavejester/hiccup

```clojure
(defn home [& [name message error]]
 (layout/common
   [:h1 "Guestbook"]
   [:p "Welcome to my guestbook"]
   [:p error]
   ;here we call our show-guests function
   ;to generate the list of existing comments
   (show-guests)
   [:hr]
   ;here we create a form with text fields called "name" and "message"
   ;these will be sent when the form posts to the server as keywords of
   ;the same name
   (form-to [:post "/"]
     [:p "Name:"]
     (text-field "name" name)
     [:p "Message:"]
     (text-area {:rows 10 :cols 40} "message" message)
     [:br]
     (submit-button "comment"))))
```

When we navigate to the browser we can see the test messages displayed along with the form. Notice that the home function now takes several optional parameters. We'll render the values of these parameters on the page. When the parameters are nil they will be rendered as empty strings.

The form we created sends an HTTP POST to the "/" route, so let's add a route to handle this action. This route will call a helper function called save-message, which we'll define shortly.

guestbook/src/guestbook/routes/home.clj
```clojure
(defroutes home-routes
 (GET "/" [] (home))
 (POST "/" [name message] (save-message name message)))
```

The save-message function will check that name and message parameters are set, then call the home function. When both parameters are supplied the message will be printed to the console; otherwise, an error message will be generated.

```clojure
(defn save-message [name message]
 (cond
   (empty? name)
   (home name message "Some dummy forgot to leave a name")
   (empty? message)
   (home name message "Don't you have something to say?")
   :else
   (do
     (println name message)
     (home))))
```

Try adding a comment in the guestbook to see that the name and the message are printed in the console. Next, try leaving the name or the message blank and see if an error is rendered.

We've now added the ability to view and submit messages from the UI. However, we don't really have anywhere to store these messages at the moment.

Adding the Data Model

Since our application will need to store the comments visitors post, let's add the JDBC and SQLite dependencies to our project.clj.[11] The :dependencies section of our project should look like the following, with the new dependencies added.

```
:dependencies [[org.clojure/clojure "1.5.1"]
               [compojure "1.1.5"]
               [hiccup "1.0.4"]
               [ring-server "0.3.0"]
               ;;JDBC dependencies
               [org.clojure/java.jdbc "0.2.3"]
               [org.xerial/sqlite-jdbc "3.7.2"]]
```

Since we've added new dependencies we'll need to reconnect our project to the REPL. To do this, navigate to the Connect tab and click the Disconnect button, then follow the previously detailed steps to connect a new REPL instance (shown in Figure 10, *Disconnecting the REPL*, on page 16).

Once we reconnect the REPL we'll need to run (start-server) in the Instarepl, as we did earlier.

We're now ready to create a model for our application. We'll create a new namespace under the src/guestbook/models folder. We'll call this namespace guestbook.models.db. To do that, right-click on the models folder in the workspace and choose the New File option. When the file is created name it db.clj.

As the name implies, the db namespace will govern the model for our application and provide functions to store and read the data from the database.

First, we'll need to add the namespace declaration and reference the database dependencies. We'll do this by writing the following namespace declaration:

guestbook/src/guestbook/models/db.clj
```
(ns guestbook.models.db
  (:require [clojure.java.jdbc :as sql])
  (:import java.sql.DriverManager))
```

---

11. http://www.sqlite.org/

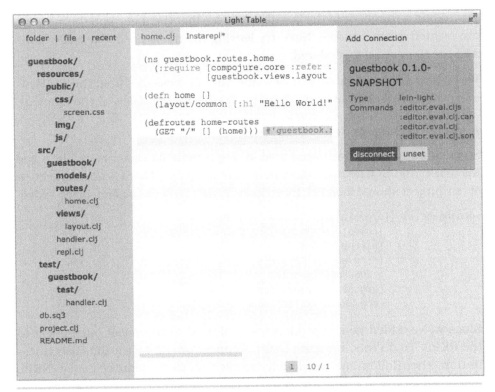

Figure 10—Disconnecting the REPL

Notice that we use the :require keyword to reference other Clojure namespaces, but we have to use :import to reference the Java classes.

Next, we'll create the definition for our database connection. The definition is simply a map containing the class for the JDBC driver, the protocol, and the name of the database file used by SQLite.

guestbook/src/guestbook/models/db.clj
```
(def db {:classname  "org.sqlite.JDBC",
         :subprotocol  "sqlite",
         :subname      "db.sq3"})
```

Now that we have a database connection declared, let's write a function to create the table for storing the guest messages.

guestbook/src/guestbook/models/db.clj
```
(defn create-guestbook-table []
  (sql/with-connection
    db
    (sql/create-table
      :guestbook
```

```
    [:id "INTEGER PRIMARY KEY AUTOINCREMENT"]
    [:timestamp "TIMESTAMP DEFAULT CURRENT_TIMESTAMP"]
    [:name "TEXT"]
    [:message "TEXT"])
  (sql/do-commands "CREATE INDEX timestamp_index ON guestbook (timestamp)")))
```

This function uses the with-connection statement, which ensures that the database connection is properly cleaned up after use. Inside it, we call the create-table function and pass it the key representing the table name, followed by vectors representing the table columns. Just to be thorough, we'll create an index on the timestamp field.

To run (create-guestbook-table) in the Instarepl we first have to reference the namespace, as we did with the guestbook.routes.home earlier.

```
(use 'guestbook.models.db)
```

```
(create-guestbook-table)
```

You should now be able to run (create-guestbook-table) in the Instarepl to create the table. If you have the *live* mode enabled you'll want to disable it before doing this. Otherwise create-guest-book-table will be called any time the scratch buffer is updated and produce errors.

With the table created, we can write a function to read the messages from the database.

guestbook/src/guestbook/models/db.clj
```
(defn read-guests []
  (sql/with-connection
    db
    (sql/with-query-results res
      ["SELECT * FROM guestbook ORDER BY timestamp DESC"]
      (doall res))))
```

Here we use with-query-results to run a select statement and return its result. The reason we call doall before returning the result is because res is lazy and doesn't load all results into memory.

By calling doall we force res to be completely evaluated. If we do not, then our connection will be closed when we leave the function scope and we won't be able to access the results outside it.

We'll also need to create a function to save new messages to our guestbook table. This function will call insert-values and pass it the name and the message to be stored as parameters.

```
guestbook/src/guestbook/models/db.clj
(defn save-message [name message]
  (sql/with-connection
    db
    (sql/insert-values
      :guestbook
      [:name :message :timestamp]
      [name message (new java.util.Date)])))
```

Now that we've written functions to read and write messages, we can try them out in the REPL. We'll need to rerun (use 'guestbook.models.db) in the Instarepl to access the newly added functions. However, both the guestbook.models.db and the guestbook.routes.home namespaces define a function called save-message.

If we try to reload the guestbook.models.db namespace we'll get an error stating that save-message has already been referenced in the guestbook.routes.home namespace. To avoid this problem we'll remove the current reference to save-message by running ns-unmap in the Instarepl before running (use 'guestbook.models.db).

```
(ns-unmap 'user 'save-message)
(use 'guestbook.models.db)
```

Now we can try running the following code and see if the logic for saving and reading messages works as expected:

```
(save-message "Bob" "hello")
(read-guests)
```

We should see the output shown in Figure 11, *Testing the save function*, on page 19 after saving a message and reading guests from our database.

With our persistence layer in place, we can go back and update our home namespace to use it instead of the dummy data we created earlier.

Putting It All Together

We'll now add the db dependency to our home route declaration.

```
guestbook/src/guestbook/routes/home.clj
(ns guestbook.routes.home
  (:require [compojure.core :refer :all]
            [guestbook.views.layout :as layout]
            [hiccup.form :refer :all]
            [guestbook.models.db :as db]))
```

Next, we'll change the show-guests function to call db/read-guests:

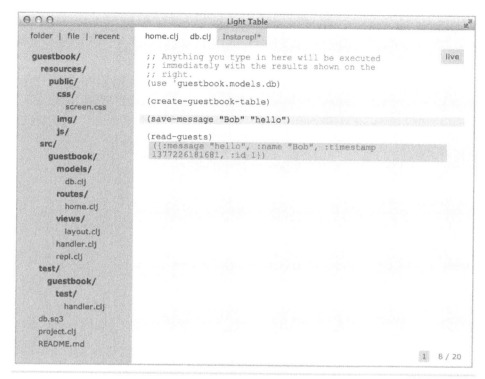

Figure 11—Testing the save function

```
(defn show-guests []
 [:ul.guests
   (for [{:keys [message name timestamp]} (db/read-guests)]
    [:li
       [:blockquote message]
       [:p "-" [:cite name]]
       [:time timestamp]])])
```

Finally, we'll change the save-message function to call db/save-message instead of printing the submitted params:

guestbook/src/guestbook/routes/home.clj
```
(defn save-message [name message]
 (cond
   (empty? name)
   (home name message "Some dummy forgot to leave a name")
   (empty? message)
   (home name message "Don't you have something to say?")
   :else
   (do
     (db/save-message name message)
     (home))))
```

With these changes in place we can navigate to our page and see that the message we added earlier in the REPL is displayed, as it is in the following figure.

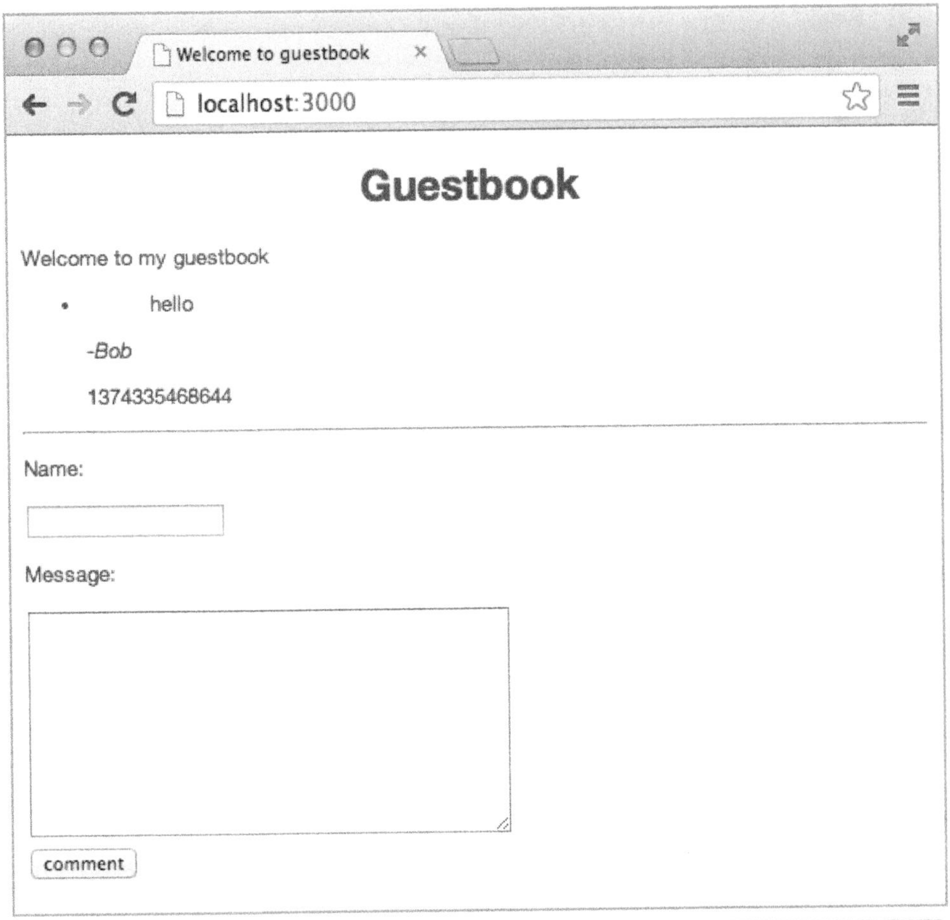

Figure 12—Working guestbook

We can now try adding more messages to confirm that our guestbook is indeed working as intended.

You've probably noticed that we still have a wart in the way we display the messages on our page. The time is simply shown as a number representing the milliseconds. This isn't terribly user-friendly, so let's add a function to format it instead.

To do that, we'll use Java interop to create an instance of SimpleDateFormat to format the timestamps for us:

```
guestbook/src/guestbook/routes/home.clj
(defn format-time [timestamp]
  (-> "dd/MM/yyyy"
      (java.text.SimpleDateFormat.)
      (.format timestamp)))
(defn show-guests []
  [:ul.guests
    (for [{:keys [message name timestamp]} (db/read-guests)]
      [:li
        [:blockquote message]
        [:p "-" [:cite name]]
        [:time (format-time timestamp)]])])
```

Finishing Touches

We're almost done building our guestbook. There's only one thing left to do.

Since we need to have the database table created in order to access it, we'll add the code for doing that to our handler namespace. First, we'll reference our db namespace in the declaration of our handler.

```
(ns guestbook.handler
  ...
  (:require ...
            [guestbook.models.db :as db]))
```

Then we'll update our init function to check whether the database exists and try to create the guestbook table if needed.

```
guestbook/src/guestbook/handler.clj
(defn init []
  (println "guestbook is starting")
  (if-not (.exists (java.io.File. "./db.sq3"))
    (db/create-guestbook-table)))
```

Since the init function runs once on load, it ensures that the database is available before we start using the application.

What Did We Just Do?

The preceding example gives us a taste of what to expect when developing web applications with Clojure. You might have noticed that you need to write very little code to get a working application. The code that you do write has little to no boilerplate.

At this point you should feel comfortable with the application's structure, its major components, and how they all fit together.

As you'll recall, the application consists of the following namespaces.

There is the guestbook.handler namespace responsible for bootstrapping and creating the handler the server uses to pass the client requests to the application.

Next we have the guestbook.routes.home namespace. This is where we set up the workflows for the actual functionality and where the bulk of application logic lives. As you add more workflows you would create new namespaces under guestbook.routes. For example, you might have a guestbook.routes.auth namespace, where you would handle user registration and authentication.

Each namespace under routes will typically encapsulate a self-contained workflow in the application. All the code pertaining to it can be found in one place and will work independently from the other routes. A workflow might represent handling user authentication, editing content, or performing administration.

The guestbook.views.layout namespace manages the application layout. Here is where we put the code to generate the common page elements and govern the structure for the pages in our application. The layout generally takes care of including static resources, such as CSS and JavaScript files the pages need, as well as setting up other common elements like headers and footers.

Finally, we have the guestbook.models.db namespace. This namespace governs the data model for the application. The table definitions will dictate the data types, and what data you persist from the client.

As we move on to build larger applications these things will remain constant. A properly structured Clojure application is easy to understand and maintain. This is great news for your application's overall life cycle, as you never have to navigate complex hierarchies like you often do when dealing with large code bases in some other languages.

We developed our application using the Light Table development environment. Although it's easy to use, it's still rough around the edges and lacks some useful features available in other integrated development environments (IDEs). These features include code completion, structural code editing, and integrated dependency management.

At this point I encourage you to take the time to try out a more mature environment such as Eclipse or Emacs.[12,13] The rest of the book will assume Eclipse as the development environment; however, it should be easy to follow

---

12. http://www.eclipse.org/
13. http://www.gnu.org/software/emacs/

regardless of the editor you're using. To see the instructions for setting up an alternative IDE, please refer to Appendix 1, *Alternative IDE Options*, on page 177.

You'll notice that we actively use the REPL while developing the application. This is different from most development environments, where the REPL is not integrated with the editor. Being able to execute code in the REPL makes you more productive by providing you with a faster feedback cycle.

In this chapter we set up our development environment and covered how a typical Clojure web application is structured. In the next chapter, we'll look at the core libraries that comprise the Clojure web stack. You'll learn about the request/response life cycle, defining routes, session management, and use of middleware to augment the core request-handling functionality.

CHAPTER 2

Clojure Web Stack

In the last chapter we jumped right into building a simple application. This let us get comfortable with the development environment and provided a glimpse at what to expect in terms of project structure. At this point we'll step back and take the time to understand how all the components work in detail.

Because the Clojure community values simplicity and flexibility, things tend not to be monolithic or prescriptive. Practically all the components of the web stack have a number of alternatives. You can pick and choose the ones that fit your style and the type of application you're developing. In this book we'll focus on the popular Ring/Compojure stack that's well established and has been used to build many real-world applications.

The previous chapter introduced a simple application that allows users to leave messages and view those left by others. We covered the directory layout and the files found in the project, as well as their purpose. However, we didn't focus very closely on the code in these files. In this chapter, you'll learn the background necessary to fully understand our guestbook application.

Since the Clojure web stack is built on top of the Java HTTP Servlet application programming interface (API),[1] applications can be deployed on any servlet container, such as Jetty, GlassFish, or Tomcat.[2,3,4]

Clojure applications can be run standalone or can be deployed side-by-side with existing Java applications using an application server.

---

1. http://www.oracle.com/technetwork/java/index-jsp-135475.html
2. http://www.eclipse.org/jetty/
3. https://glassfish.java.net/
4. http://tomcat.apache.org/

Since many cloud services run on the Java Virtual Machine, you would be able to deploy your applications there, as well. Such services include Amazon Web Services, Google App Engine, Heroku, and Jelastic.[5,6,7,8]

A servlet receives requests and generates corresponding responses based on the HTTP protocol specification. The API provides many of the core features needed in a web application, such as cookies, sessions, and URL rewriting. However, servlets are designed to be used from Java, and using them directly from Clojure does not provide the best experience for the user.

Unlike many platforms, such as Rails or Django, the Clojure web stack does not offer a single opinionated framework. Instead, you can put together a number of libraries to build your application. In this book we'll focus on several libraries commonly used for web development.

We'll start by looking at the Clojure libraries that provide the native Clojure API for working with servlets. These libraries are called Ring and Compojure. Ring acts as a wrapper around Java servlets. In turn, Compojure uses it to map request-handler functions to specific URLs. The application sits on top of this stack, using these libraries to interact with the client and manage the application state.

Routing Requests with Ring

Ring aims to abstract the details of HTTP into a simple and modular API that can be used to build a large spectrum of applications. If you've developed web applications in Python or Ruby, then you'll find it similar to the WSGI and Rack libraries found in those languages.[9,10]

Since Ring has become the de facto standard for building web applications, a lot of tools and middleware have been developed around it. While in most cases you won't need to use Ring directly, it's useful to have a high-level understanding of its design, as it will help you in developing and troubleshooting your applications.

Ring applications consist of four basic components: the *handler*, the *request*, the *response*, and the *middleware*. Let's look at each one of these.

---

5. http://aws.amazon.com/
6. https://developers.google.com/appengine/
7. https://www.heroku.com/
8. http://jelastic.com/
9. http://wsgi.readthedocs.org/en/latest/
10. http://rack.github.io/

Handling Requests

Ring uses standard Clojure maps to represent the client requests and the responses returned by the server. The handlers are functions that process the incoming requests. They accept request maps and return response maps. A very simple Ring handler might look like this:

```
(defn handler [request-map]
  {:status 200

   :headers {"Content-Type" "text/html"}
   :body (str "<html><body> your IP is: "
              (:remote-addr request-map)
              "</body></html>")})
```

As you can see, it accepts a map representing an HTTP request and returns a map representing an HTTP response. Ring then takes care of generating an HTTP servlet request, and response objects from these maps.

The preceding handler simply serves an HTML string with the client's IP address and sets the response status to 200. Since this is a common operation, the Ring API provides a helper function for generating such responses:

```
(defn handler [request-map]
  (response

    (str "<html><body> your IP is: "
         (:remote-addr request-map)
         "</body></html>")))
```

If you wanted to create a custom response, you'd simply have to write a function that would accept a request map, and return a response map representing your custom response. Let's look at the format for the request and response maps.

Request and Response Maps

The request and response maps will contain information such as the server port, URI, remote address, and content type, plus the body with the actual payload. The keys in these maps are based on the servlet API and the official HTTP RFC.[11]

What's in the Request Map

The request defines the following standard keys. Note that not all of these keys, such as :ssl-client-cert, are guaranteed to be present in a request.

---

11. http://www.w3.org/Protocols/rfc2616/rfc2616.html

- :server-port — The port on which the server is handling the request.

- :server-name — The server's IP address or the name it resolves to.

- :remote-addr — The client's IP address.

- :query-string — The request's query string.

- :scheme — The specifier of the protocol, which can be either :http or :https.

- :request-method — The HTTP request method, such as :get, :head, :options, :put, :post, or :delete.

- :request-string — The request's query string.

- :content-type — The request body's MIME type.

- :content-length — The number of bytes in the request.

- :character-encoding — The name of the request's character encoding.

- :headers — A map containing the request headers.

- :body — An input stream for the body of the request.

- :context — The context in which the application can be found when not deployed as root.

- :uri — The request URI path on the server; this string will have the :context prepended when available.

- :ssl-client-cert — The client's SSL certificate.

In addition to the standard keys from the Ring specification, it is possible to use middleware functions to extend the request map with other application-specific keys. Later in this chapter we'll cover how to accomplish this.

What's in the Response Map

The response map contains only three keys needed to describe the HTTP response:

- :status — The response's HTTP status
- :headers — Any HTTP headers to be returned to the client
- :body — The response's body

The status is a number representing one of the status codes specified in the HTTP RFC, the lowest allowed number being 100.

The header is a map containing the HTTP-header key/value pairs. Headers may be strings or a sequence of strings, in which case a key and a value will be sent for each string in the sequence.

Finally, the response body can contain either a string, a sequence, a file, or an input stream. The body must correspond appropriately with the response's status code.

When the response body is a string, it will be sent back to the client as is. If it is a sequence, then a string representing each element is sent to the client. Finally, if the response is a file or an input stream, then the server sends its contents to the client.

Adding Functionality with Middleware

The middleware allows wrapping the handlers in functions that can modify the way the request is processed. Middleware functions are often used to extend the base functionality of Ring handlers to match your application's needs.

A middleware handler is a function that accepts an existing handler with some optional parameters, then returns a new handler with some added behavior. The following is an example of such a function:

```
(defn handler [request]
  (response
    (str "<html><body> your IP is: "
         (:remote-addr request)
         "</body></html>")))

(defn wrap-nocache [handler]
  (fn [request]
    (let [response (handler request)]
      (assoc-in response [:headers  "Pragma"] "no-cache"))))

(def app (wrap-nocache handler))
```

The wrapper in our example accepts the handler and returns a function that in turn acts as a handler. Since the returned function was defined in the local scope, it can reference the handler internally. When invoked, it will call the handler with the request and add Pragma: no-cache to the response map.

The wrapper function is called a closure because it closes over the handler parameter and makes it accessible to the function it returns.

The technique we've just seen allows us to create small functions, each dealing with a particular aspect of the application. We can then easily chain them together to provide complex behaviors needed for real-world applications.

What Are the Adapters?

Adapters sit between the handlers and the underlying HTTP protocol. They provide any necessary configuration, such as port mappings, and handle parsing HTTP requests into request maps and constructing HTTP responses from the handler response maps. You will generally not need to interact with adapters directly. We won't say anything more about them.

Defining the Routes with Compojure

Compojure is a routing library built on top of Ring. It provides an easy way to associate handler functions with a URL and an HTTP method. A Compojure route might look like this:

```
(GET "/:id" [id] (str "<p>the id is: " id "</p>" ))
```

The route name maps to an HTTP method name, such as GET, POST, PUT, DELETE, or HEAD. There's also a route called ANY that matches any method the client supplies. The URI can contain keys denoted by using a colon, and their values can be used as parameters to the route. This feature was inspired by a similar mechanism used in Rails and Sinatra.[12,13] The route's response will be automatically wrapped in the Ring response described earlier.

Since we're likely to have more than a single route in our application, Compojure provides the routes function that creates a Ring handler from multiple routes. For example, if we had routes /all-items and item/:id, then we could combine these into a single handler as follows:

```
(defn foo-handler []
  "foo called")

(defn bar-handler [id]
  (str "bar called, id is: " id))

(def handler
  (routes
    (GET "/foo" []        (foo-handler))
    (GET "/bar/:id" [id] (bar-handler id))))
```

Since defining routes is a very common operation, Compojure also provides the defroutes macro that generates a Ring handler from the supplied routes:

```
(defroutes handler
  (GET "/foo" []        (foo-handler))
  (GET "/bar/:id" [id] (bar-handler id)))
```

---

12. http://rubyonrails.org/
13. http://www.sinatrarb.com/

Using Compojure routes, we can easily map functionality to each URL of our site, and provide much of the core functionality needed in a web application. We can then group these routes together using the defroutes macro as we did previously. Compojure, in turn, takes care of creating the Ring handlers.

Compojure also provides a powerful mechanism for filtering out common routes in the application based on the shared path elements. Let's say we have several routes that handle operations for a specific user:

```
(defn display-profile [id]
  ;;TODO: display user profile
  )
(defn display-settings [id]
  ;;TODO: display user account settings
  )
(defn change-password [id]
  ;;TODO: display the page for setting a new password
  )
(defroutes user-routes
  (GET "/user/:id/profile" [id] (display-profile id))
  (GET "/user/:id/settings" [id] (display-settings id))
  (GET "/user/:id/change-password" [id] (change-password-page id)))
```

There's a lot of repetition in that code, where each route starts with the /user/:id segment. We can use the context macro to factor out the common portion of these routes:

```
(def user-routes
    (context "/user/:id" [id]
       (GET "/profile" [] (display-profile id))
       (GET "/settings" [] (display-settings id))
       (GET "/change-password" [] (change-password-page id))))
```

In that code the routes defined in the context of /user/:id will behave exactly the same as the previous version and have access to the id parameter. The context macro exploits the fact that handlers are closures. When the outer context handler closes over the common parameters, they are also available to handlers defined inside it.

Accessing Request Parameters

For some routes, we'll need to access the request map to access the request parameters. We do this by declaring the map as the second argument to the route.

```
(GET "/foo" request (interpose ", " (keys request)))
```

That route reads out all the keys from the request map and displays them. The output will look like the following.

```
:ssl-client-cert, :remote-addr, :scheme, :query-params, :session, :form-params,
:multipart-params, :request-method, :query-string, :route-params, :content-type,
:cookies, :uri, :server-name, :params, :headers, :content-length, :server-port,
:character-encoding, :body, :flash
```

Compojure also provides some useful functionality for handling the request maps and the form parameters. For example, in the guestbook application, which we created in Chapter 1, *Getting Your Feet Wet*, on page 1, we saw the following route defined:

```
(POST "/" [name message] (save-message name message))
```

This route extracts the :name and :message keys from the request params, then binds them to variables of the same name. We can now use them as any other declared variable within the route's scope.

It's also possible to use the regular Clojure destructuring inside the route. Given a request map containing the following parameters...

```
{:params {"name" "some value"}}
```

...we can extract the parameter with the key "name" as follows:

```
(GET "/:foo" {{value "name"} :params}
  (str "The value of name is " value))
```

Furthermore, Compojure lets you destructure a subset of form parameters and create a map from the rest:

```
[x y & z]
x -> "foo"
y -> "bar"
z -> {:v "baz", :w "qux"}
```

In the preceding code, parameters x and y have been bound to variables, while parameters v and w remain in a map called z. Finally, if we need to get at the complete request along with the parameters, we can do the following:

```
(GET "/" [x y :as r] (str x y r))
```

Here we bind the form parameters x and y, and bind the complete request map to the variable r.

Armed with the functionality that Ring and Compojure provide, we can easily create pages and routes for our site. However, any nontrivial application requires many other features, such as page templating, session management, and input validation. For these tasks we'll use the libraries best adapted for each task.

Application Architecture

The approach that a typical Compojure web application takes is probably different from what you're used to. Most frameworks favor using the model-view-controller (MVC) pattern for partitioning the application logic with strong separation between the view, the controller, and the model. Compojure does not enforce any strict separation between the view and the controller.

Instead, we create handlers for each application route. The handler processes HTTP requests from the client and dispatches actions based on them. The handlers drive the model that's responsible for handling the domain logic. This approach provides a clean separation between the domain logic and the presentation layer of your application without introducing any unnecessary indirection.

However, since the Clojure web stack is designed to be flexible, it will ultimately let you design the site any way you like. If you do feel strongly about having a traditional-style MVC in your application, there's nothing stopping you from doing that.

A typical application would be broken up into several logical components (mentioned when we discussed the structure of the guestbook application). Let's look at these in some more detail. The major components that will be present in most applications are as follows:

- hanlder — This namespace is responsible for handling requests and responses.

- routes — The routes contain the core of our application, such as the logic to render pages and handle client requests.

- model — This namespace is reserved for the data model of the application and the persistence layer.

- views — This namespace contains common logic for generating the application layout.

Application Handler

The handler is the entry point for the application. It is typically defined in the handler namespace. It is responsible for aggregating all the routes for the application and defining any application-handler functions wrapped with any necessary middleware.

The handler namespace also defines some base routes for the application that aren't related to any specific workflows. In the handler from the guestbook application, we have two routes: a route for static resources and a catch-all route for handling request URIs that haven't been defined.

```
(defroutes app-routes
  (route/resources "/")
  (route/not-found "Not Found"))
```

Routes related to specific workflows, such as posting and viewing messages in the guestbook, are grouped in their own namespaces. The application-specific namespaces, in turn, live under the routes namespace.

The handler namespace also provides the init and destroy functions. These are called when the application starts and shuts down. Any code that needs to be run on startup or shutdown should be called from these functions, respectively.

One example of using an init function would be to check whether the database connection is available, as we did with our guestbook application.

```
(defn init []
  (println "guestbook is starting")
  (if-not (.exists (java.io.File. "./db.sq3"))
    (db/create-guestbook-table)))
```

Next, we define the entry point, called app, through which all the requests to our application will be routed.

```
(def app (handler/site (routes home-routes app-routes)))
```

In that code, the compojure.handler/site function is used to generate a Ring handler wrapped in middleware suitable for a typical website.

The site function simply creates a handler wrapped in some common middleware that is suitable for a common website. This middleware consists of the following wrappers:

- wrap-session
- wrap-flash
- wrap-cookies
- wrap-multipart-params
- wrap-params
- wrap-nested-params
- wrap-keyword-params

The application handler, init function, and destroy function are bound in the project.clj under the :ring key. We can see an example of this in our guestbook application from Chapter 1, *Getting Your Feet Wet*, on page 1.

```
:ring {:handler guestbook.handler/app
       :init    guestbook.handler/init
       :destroy guestbook.handler/destroy}
```

This is all there is to bootstrapping the application core. Now let's see how we can add some routes to provide the functionality specific to our application.

Routing Requests

As we discussed earlier, application routes represent URIs that the client can call to cause the server to perform an action. Each route is mapped to a particular function that will be called when the client requests the URI associated with it.

Any real-world applications will require more than a single route. For example, in our guestbook application we had two separate routes, each performing a distinct action:

guestbook/src/guestbook/routes/home.clj
```
(defroutes home-routes
  (GET "/" [] (home))
  (POST "/" [name message] (save-message name message)))
```

The first route was bound to / and would retrieve the messages from the database and render a page displaying them alongside a form for creating a new message.

The second route would handle the user input. If the input turns out to be valid, then the message is stored in the database; otherwise the page is rendered with an accompanying error.

Since both of these routes have related functionality—storing and displaying user messages—they are considered to be part of the same workflow.

When you identify a specific workflow in your application, it makes sense to group all the logic relating to this workflow in a single place. The routes package in your application is reserved for the namespaces that describe these workflows.

Since our guestbook application is very small, we define a single set of routes, along with some helper functions right in the guestbook.routes.home namespace.

In an application that has more pages, we would want to create additional namespaces to keep the code manageable. We would then create separate routes under each namespace and group them together in the handler namespace using the routes macro Compojure provides.

The routes macro will combine all the routes into a single set from which the final handler can be created. Be aware that routes can mask other routes. Since our app-routes contains (route/not-found "Not Found"), we should put it last, or the not-found route will prevent any routes defined after it from resolving.

Application Model

All but the most trivial applications need some sort of a model. The model describes the data stored by the application and interrelations between individual data elements. In our guestbook application, the model consists of a user table and a messages table.

All namespaces dealing with the model and the persistence layer traditionally live under the application's models package. We'll focus on this fairly large topic in the next chapter.

Application Views

The views package is reserved for providing the visual layouts and other common elements for our pages. It comes prepopulated with the layout namespace. This namespace includes the common layout declaration to take care of generating the base page template for us.

The common layout adds the head and title tags, includes resources such as CSS, and appends the content to the body. Since the content is wrapped using the html5 macro, an HTML string is automatically generated from the content when the common layout is called. This handler will then serve the string back to the client.

It's idiomatic to create a common layout that provides the basic page structure and use it to define the individual pages. This way all the common page elements, such as headers, footers, and menus, can be kept in one place. Any time we create a page we'll simply wrap its body with the layout we defined.

Defining Pages

The pages are defined by creating routes that accept the request parameters and generate the appropriate response. A route can return HTML markup, perform a server-side operation, redirect to a different page, or return a specific type of data, such as a JavaScript Object Notation (JSON) string or a file.

In many cases a page will have multiple route components. One route responds to GET requests and returns HTML to be rendered by the browser. The rest handle events such as form submissions generated by the client when the user interacts with the page.

The page body can be generated by any means we choose, and Compojure is agnostic as to the method we use. This leaves us with the option of using any templating library we like, and there are several to choose from. Some popular choices are Hiccup, Enlive, Selmer, and Stencil.[14,15,16,17]

Hiccup simply uses Clojure data structures to define the markup and generates the corresponding HTML from it. Enlive takes the opposite approach of defining pages using pure HTML without the use of any special processing tags. The HTML templates are then transformed by adapters specific to your models and domains.

Unlike Hiccup and Enlive, Stencil and Selmer are based on the existing templating systems that aren't rooted in Clojure. Stencil is an implementation of Mustache, which is a popular logicless templating system. Selmer is modeled on the Django template system from Python.

In this book we'll primarily focus on using Hiccup because it doesn't necessitate learning any special syntax outside of using standard Clojure functions. However, later on you'll see how to transform an application written using Hiccup to use Selmer templates instead.

Another option is to not do any server-side templating at all. Instead you could use one of many popular JavaScript libraries to do the templating on the client and communicate with the server using Ajax. This provides a clean separation between your application's client and server components. It also facilitates using other clients with the server, such as native mobile interfaces. This approach is particularly popular when writing single-page applications.[18]

Regardless of your favorite templating strategy, it's good practice not to mix domain logic with views. In a properly designed application it should be relatively easy to swap out one templating engine for another.

Page Templating with Hiccup

We'll now look at some of the basics of using Hiccup and exactly how page elements are generated from it.

As I mentioned previously, Hiccup templates are written in plain Clojure, so you don't have to learn a separate domain-specific language to use it.

---

14. https://github.com/weavejester/hiccup
15. https://github.com/cgrand/enlive
16. https://github.com/yogthos/Selmer
17. https://github.com/davidsantiago/stencil
18. http://en.wikipedia.org/wiki/Single-page_application

Hiccup uses Clojure vectors with optional maps of attributes to represent HTML elements. The structure of the element corresponds to the structure of the resulting HTML tag, as shown here:

```
[:tag-name {:attribute-key "attribute value"} tag body]
```

```
<tag-name attribute-key="attribute value">tag body</tag-name>
```

If we wanted to create a div with a paragraph in it, we could create a vector, where the first element is a keyword :div, followed by the map containing the ID and the div's class. The rest of the content consists of a vector representing the paragraph.

```
[:div {:id "hello", :class "content"} [:p "Hello world!"]]
```

To generate an HTML string from our vector, we use hiccup.core/html macro:

```
(html [:div {:id "hello", :class "content"} [:p "Hello world!"]])
```

```
<div id="hello" class="content"><p>Hello world!</p></div>
```

Because Hiccup allows you to set element attributes via the attribute map, you could style elements inline if you wanted. However, you should resist this temptation and instead use CSS for the styling of elements. This will ensure that the structure is kept separate from the presentation.

Since setting the ID and the class for elements is a very common operation, Hiccup provides CSS style shortcuts for these actions. Instead of what we wrote earlier, we could simply write our div as follows:

```
[:div#hello.content [:p "Hello world!"]]
```

Hiccup also provides a number of helper functions for defining common elements such as forms, links, and images. All of these functions output vectors in the Hiccup format described previously.

When a function doesn't do what you need, you can either write out the literal form for the element by hand or modify its output to fit your needs. Each function that describes an HTML element can also take an optional map of attributes as its first parameter. We'll now look at some of the most commonly used Hiccup helpers to get a better feel for the library.

First, let's look at the link-to helper that creates an a tag.

```
(link-to {:align "left"} "http://google.com" "google")
```

That code will produce the following vector:

```
[:a {:align "left", :href #<URI http://google.com>} ("google")]
```

There we have the keyword :a as the first item, followed by the map of attributes and a list representing the content.

Again, we can output the HTML based on this vector by wrapping our link-to function in the html macro.

```
(html (link-to  {:align "left"} "http://google.com" "google"))

<a align="left" href="http://google.com">google</a>
```

Another commonly used function is form-to, used for generating HTML forms. We used this function in the previous chapter to create a form that submits messages to the server.

```
(form-to [:post "/"]
         [:p "Name:" (text-field "name")]
         [:p "Message:" (text-area {:rows 10 :cols 40} "message")]
         (submit-button "comment"))
```

This helper takes a vector with the type of the HTTP request specified as a keyword, followed by the URL string. The rest of the arguments should evaluate to vectors representing HTML elements. The preceding code will be converted to the following HTML when the html macro is called:

```
<form action="/" method="POST">
  <p>Name:<input id="name" name="name" type="text" /></p>
  <p>Message:<textarea cols="40" id="message" name="message" rows="10">
  </textarea></p><input type="submit" value="comment" />
</form>
```

Another useful helper is the defhtml macro. With it we can define a function that will implicitly generate HTML from its body. It means we don't need to use the html macro for each individual element when constructing our pages.

```
(defhtml page [& body]
  [:html
    [:head
    [:title "Welcome"]]
    [:body body]])
```

Hiccup also provides a number of macros to produce specific HTML variants such as HTML4, HTML5, and XHTML in the hiccup.page namespace. You'll see that we used the html5 macro in our guestbook layout:

```
(defn common [& body]
  (html5
    [:head
    [:title "Welcome to guestbook"]
    (include-css "/css/screen.css")]
    [:body body]))
```

Including Resources

Any nontrivial website will, of course, include JavaScript and CSS in the pages. Hiccup provides a couple of utility functions in the hiccup.page namespace for this purpose. You can use include-css to include any CSS files, and include-js to include JavaScript resources. Here's an example of CSS and JavaScript resources being included in the common layout.

```
(defn common [& content]
  (html5
    [:head
      [:title "My App"]
      (include-css "/css/mobile.css"
                   "/css/screen.css")
      (include-js "//code.jquery.com/jquery-1.10.1.min.js"
                  "/js/uielements.js")]
    [:body content]))
```

As you can see, both include-css and include-js can accept multiple strings, each specifying a resource URI. The output of these is, of course, a Hiccup vector, which will be converted to HTML.

```
;;output of include-css
([:link
  {:type "text/css", :href #<URI /css/reset.css>, :rel "stylesheet"}]
 [:link
  {:type "text/css", :href #<URI /css/screen.css>, :rel "stylesheet"}])

;;output of include-js
([:script
  {:type "text/javascript",
   :src
   #<URI //code.jquery.com/jquery-1.10.1.min.js>}]
 [:script {:type "text/javascript", :src #<URI /js/uielements.js>}])
```

Hiccup also provides a helper for including images using the /image function found in the hiccup.element namespace:

```
(image "/img/test.jpg")
[:img {:src #<URI /img/test.jpg>}]
(image "/img/test.jpg" "alt text")
[:img {:src #<URI /img/test.jpg>, :alt "alt text"}]
```

Hiccup API Overview

You've seen some of the commonly used functions, but there are many more available. The majority of the helper functions are found under the element and form namespaces. Here we find functions for defining elements such as images, links, script tags, check boxes, drop-downs, and input fields.

As you can see, Hiccup provides a concise API for generating HTML templates in addition to the literal vector syntax. Armed with our understanding of Hiccup, let's take a closer look at the code in our guestbook application.

Revisiting the Guestbook Application

Let's start by taking another look at the functions defined in the home namespace. If you run the application and navigate to it from the browser, you can inspect and compare the output HTML to its definition.

First, we have the show-guests function to generate an unordered list with a class guests. It loops over the messages in the database and creates a list item for each message.

```
(defn show-guests []
 [:ul.guests
   (for [{:keys [message name timestamp]} (db/read-guests)]
   [:li
      [:blockquote message]
      [:p "-" [:cite name]]
      [:time (format-time timestamp)]])])
```

The function uses a helper to format each timestamp for display. This function uses the java.text.SimpleDateFormat to generate a formatted string given a date object. We use the threading macro to instantiate the formatter with the format string. We then use its instance to format the timestamp we got from the database.

```
(defn format-time [timestamp]
  (-> "dd/MM/yyyy"
      (java.text.SimpleDateFormat.)
      (.format timestamp)))
```

You'll notice that the actual home function is a bit more complicated, as it renders the existing comments in addition to providing the submision form.

Things to note here are the error paragraph used to display the value of the error key populated by the controller, and the use of the show-guests function to render the comments.

The home function generates the HTML for the page by wrapping its content with layout/common.

```
(defn home [& [name message error]]
  (layout/common
    [:h1 "Guestbook"]
    [:p "Welcome to my guestbook"]
    [:p error]
```

```
(show-guests)
[:hr]
(form-to [:post "/"]
  [:p "Name:" (text-field "name" name)]
  [:p "Message:" (text-area {:rows 10 :cols 40} "message" message)]
  (submit-button "comment"))))
```

As you can see, creating page templates using Hiccup takes very little code and produces output markup that's easy to correlate back to the template definitions.

Lastly, we have our route definitions, where Compojure routes are defined.

```
(defroutes home-routes
  (GET "/" [name message error] (home name message error))
  (POST "/" [name message] (save-message name message)))
```

Up to now all we've done is create routes to render pages and handle form parameters from the client. As we noted earlier, a real application will need a few other things on top of what Ring and Compojure provide. Let's explore how to add more functionality to our applications.

Beyond Compojure and Ring

Lots of libraries are available for doing tasks such as session management, input validation, and authentication. As always, you can pick and choose the components that are right for you.

The library we'll focus on is lib-noir.[19] It's a comprehensive suite of utilities for handling the most common operations in a web application. As we did with Hiccup, we'll focus our attention on the most commonly used features and then segue into an overview of the API.

First, we'll need to add lib-noir to our project.clj to use it. We'll do this by adding [lib-noir "0.7.6"] to our dependencies vector.

If you have your project running as you follow along, which you should be doing, then you'll need to restart it for the dependency to be picked up. Now let's see how we can use lib-noir to add some functionality to our application.

Handling Redirects

In some cases we'll want to redirect the client to another page after an action is performed. For example, if a user registers an account on the registration page, we would want to redirect the user to the home page afterward.

---

19. https://github.com/noir-clojure/lib-noir

Let's add a page that lets the user register an account on our site. We'll add the page to a new namespace called guestbook.routes.auth. The namespace will need to reference other namespaces, similar to the home namespace.

```
(ns guestbook.routes.auth
  (:require [compojure.core :refer [defroutes GET POST]]
            [guestbook.views.layout :as layout]
            [hiccup.form :refer
             [form-to label text-field password-field submit-button]]))
```

The function to render our page will have a form that asks the user to enter an ID and a password.

```
(defn registration-page []
  (layout/common
    (form-to [:post "/register"]
             (label "id" "screen name")
             (text-field "id")
             [:br]
             (label "pass" "password")
             (password-field "pass")
             [:br]
             (label "pass1" "retype password")
             (password-field "pass1")
             [:br]
             (submit-button "create account"))))
```

You'll notice that the function has a very repetitive structure. Each input needs a label and should be followed by a break. Since Hiccup uses standard Clojure data structures to represent the markup, we can trivially factor out the repeating elements into a helper function:

```
(defn control [field name text]
  (list (label name text)
        (field name)
        [:br]))

(defn registration-page []
  (layout/common
    (form-to [:post "/register"]
      (control text-field :id "screen name")
      (control password-field :pass "Password")
      (control password-field :pass1 "Retype Password")
      (submit-button "Create Account"))))
```

In that code we use the list function instead of making a vector as we normally would. This is because Hiccup uses vectors to represent HTML tags and the tag content cannot itself be a vector.

To make our new page available to the client, we'll have to define a new route for it. We'll wrap it in a route definition called auth-routes.

```
(defroutes auth-routes
  (GET "/register" [_] (registration-page)))
```

The underscore (_) in the user page's arguments vector is simply a convention to indicate that the function won't use the argument.

Since we created a new set of routes, we'll need to update our app handler with them as well. To do that we'll have to reference the new namespace in our handler namespace declaration and add the routes to our app definition, as shown here.

```
(ns guestbook.handler
  ...
  (:require ...
    [guestbook.routes.auth :refer [auth-routes]]))


...

(def app
  (handler/site
    (routes auth-routes home-routes app-routes)))
```

Note that new routes should be added before app-routes, as the (route/not-found "Not Found") route is defined there. This route will mask any other routes defined after it.

If you have the site running in the REPL, then you'll need to restart it to pick up the new routes.

Once the site is restarted, navigate to http://localhost:3000/register to confirm that the page loads correctly. If all went well, we can add the handler for the registration page.

The handler will redirect the user to the home page upon successful registration. A redirect is simply a map containing the status, headers, and body:

```
{:status 302, :headers {"Location" "/"}, :body ""}
```

Ring provides a redirect function in its ring.util.response namespace. Since we're already using lib-noir, we'll use noir.response/redirect instead. The version from lib-noir allows specifying an optional key indicating the redirect's status code. It defaults to :found, corresponding to the redirect code 302.

We'll need to reference this namespace to access it, so let's add it to the :require section of the auth namespace.

```
(ns guestbook.routes.auth
  (:require ...
            [noir.response :refer [redirect]]]))
```

Now we can add our handler to the auth-routes definition. At the moment we'll simply check if the entered passwords match, and redirect to the home page. Otherwise we'll render the page again.

```
(defroutes auth-routes
  (GET "/register" [] (registration-page))
  (POST "/register" [id pass pass1]
        (if (= pass pass1)
          (redirect "/")
          (registration-page))))
```

Managing Sessions

When users interact with our application we need a way to keep track of each user session's state. Luckily, lib-noir provides a way to manage sessions via its noir.session namespace. A client session is represented by a map that can be accessed using the following helper functions:

- clear! — Clears everything from the session
- flash-put — Stores a value for a single retrieval
- flash-get — Retrieves a flash-stored value and clears it
- get — Gets a value from the session
- put! — Puts a value in session
- remove! — Removes a value from session

The functions used to change the session's state are marked with an exclamation point (!), as per Clojure convention for indicating in-place mutation. Let's look at an example where we'll implement *login* and *logout* pages. Each of these actions should update the session accordingly.

To use lib-noir sessions we'll have to wrap the app handler with the session middleware. This is needed because the original handler is not aware of sessions and doesn't provide a method for persisting state between requests.

The middleware requires that we provide a store where the session state will be persisted. This could be in-memory or backed by an external store such as Redis.[20]

We'll simply use the ring.middleware.session.memory/memory-store for our application. Both the middleware and the store will first have to be referenced in the namespace declaration.

---

20. http://redis.io/

```
(ns guestbook.handler
  ...
  (:require ...
    [noir.session :as session]
    [ring.middleware.session.memory
      :refer [memory-store]]))
```

Next, we'll wrap our app using the session middleware. The wrap-noir-session middleware accepts a map of parameters containing the :store key. We bind this key to the memory-store.

```
(def app
  (->
    (handler/site
      (routes auth-routes
              home-routes
              app-routes))
    (session/wrap-noir-session
      {:store (memory-store)})))
```

Now let's see what's involved in creating a login page and adding the user to the session. Let's navigate to the auth namespace and add the following function to it.

```
(defn login-page []
  (layout/common
    (form-to [:post "/login"]
      (control text-field :id "screen name")
      (control password-field :pass "Password")
      (submit-button "login"))))
```

The function creates a login form that collects the user ID and the password, and wraps it using the common layout. The form will do an HTTP post to the /login URI when the Submit button is clicked.

We'll now update our route definitions to create the GET and POST /login routes for our application. We'll also have to reference the noir.session for our routes to work.

```
(ns guestbook.routes.auth
  (:require ...
            [noir.session :as session]))
...

(defroutes auth-routes
  (GET "/register" [] (registration-page))
  (POST "/register" [id pass pass1]
        (if (= pass pass1)
          (redirect "/")
          (registration-page))))
```

```
(GET "/login" [] (login-page))
(POST "/login" [id pass]
      (session/put! :user id)
      (redirect "/")))
```

The GET login route simply calls the login-page function to render the page. The POST login route uses the noir.session/put! function to add the user to the session with the key :user before redirecting to the home page. Now we can navigate to /login in our browser and try out the functionality we've added.

To see that the user is in session, we'd have to update our home page to display the user ID. We can do this by calling (session/get :user) when our home function renders the page. As usual, we'll have to remember to include a reference to noir.session in our home namespace declaration.

```
(ns guestbook.routes.home
  (:require ... [noir.session :as session])
```

guestbook-with-auth/src/guestbook/routes/home.clj
```
(defn home [& [name message error]]
  (layout/common
    [:h1 "Guestbook " (session/get :user)]
    [:p "Welcome to my guestbook"]
    [:p error]

    (show-guests)

    [:hr]

    (form-to [:post "/"]
             [:p "Name:" (text-field "name" name)]
             [:p "Message:" (text-area {:rows 10 :cols 40} "message" message)]
             (submit-button "comment"))))
```

Next we'll create the logout page to call noir.session/clear!. When the user clicks the logout button, this will purge any information that was accumulated during the session.

```
(defroutes auth-routes
  (GET "/register" [] (registration-page))
  (POST "/register" [id pass pass1]
        (if (= pass pass1)
          (redirect "/")
          (registration-page)))

  (GET "/login" [] (login-page))
  (POST "/login" [id pass]
        (session/put! :user id)
        (redirect "/"))
```

```clojure
(GET "/logout" []
     (layout/common
       (form-to [:post "/logout"]
         (submit-button "logout"))))
(POST "/logout" []
      (session/clear!)
      (redirect "/")))
```

Keep in mind that the session namespace must be accessed within the context of a request, meaning that it should not be used outside the scope of a route declaration.

Handling Input Validation

When creating forms, we need a way to check if they have been filled out correctly and to notify the user about missing or improperly completed fields. Up to now we've simply been populating an error key in our parameters and displaying it on the page.

Continuing with that approach, we would use the cond statement to decide whether to render the login page with an error or put the user in session and redirect:

```clojure
(defn login-page [& [error]]
  (layout/common
    (if error [:div.error "Login error: " error])
    (form-to [:post "/login"]
      (control text-field :id "screen name")
      (control password-field :pass "Password")
      (submit-button "login"))))

(defn handle-login [id pass]
  (cond
    (empty? id)
    (login-page "screen name is required")
    (empty? pass)
    (login-page "password is required")
    (and (= "foo" id) (= "bar" pass))
    (do
      (session/put! :user id)
      (redirect "/"))

    :else
    (login-page "authentication failed")))
```

Next, we update our POST /login route to use the handle-login function as its handler.

```clojure
(POST "/login" [id pass]
  (handle-login id pass))
```

Although this approach works for simple cases, it would quickly become tedious to do for more complex sets of rules. Once again, lib-noir provides an excellent way to handle input validation using the noir.validation namespace. Let's reference it in our auth namespace and see how we can improve our validation using it.

```
(ns guestbook.routes.auth
  (:require ...
            [noir.validation
             :refer [rule errors? has-value? on-error]]))
```

To use the validation functions, we'll also have to wrap our handler in wrap-noir-validation middleware. To do that we'll require noir.validation in the handler namespace.

```
(ns guestbook.handler
  ...
  (:require ...
            [noir.validation
             :refer [wrap-noir-validation]]))
```

guestbook-with-auth/src/guestbook/handler.clj
```
(def app
  (->
    (handler/site
      (routes auth-routes
              home-routes
              app-routes))
    (wrap-base-url)
    (session/wrap-noir-session
      {:store (memory-store)})
    (wrap-noir-validation)))
```

If you're following along with the REPL, then you'll need to reload the application to recompile the routes.

Instead of using a cond statement, we now use the noir.validation/rule helper. Each rule is checked independently to see whether it passes. At the end of the function we call noir.validation/errors? to check if any of the rules have set an error. If so, we render the login page; otherwise we put the user in the session and redirect to the home page.

```
(defn handle-login [id pass]
  (rule (has-value? id)
        [:id "screen name is required"])
  (rule (= id "foo")
        [:id "unknown user"])
  (rule (has-value? pass)
        [:pass "password is required"])
```

```
(rule (= pass "bar")
      [:pass "invalid password"])

(if (errors? :id :pass)
  (login-page)

  (do
    (session/put! :user id)
    (redirect "/"))))
```

Each of the rules we created has the following form:

```
(rule validator [:field-name "error message"])
```

The validator can be any expression that evaluates to a Boolean value. It is also possible to set multiple errors for each key; these will all be aggregated into an error vector. The error is generated when the validator returns false.

For example, when we say (= id "foo"), the error will be generated when the id field has any value other than foo.

Because we set only a single error per item, we create a helper for grabbing it and displaying the paragraph with the error.

guestbook-with-auth/src/guestbook/routes/auth.clj
```
(defn format-error [[error]]
  [:p.error error])
```

We now update the control function to call on-error with the name of the control. It will grab the errors for the supplied key and use the format-error to format them.

guestbook-with-auth/src/guestbook/routes/auth.clj
```
(defn control [field name text]
  (list (on-error name format-error)
        (label name text)
        (field name)
        [:br]))
```

Since we no longer need to pass the error directly to the login-page, we'll update it accordingly.

guestbook-with-auth/src/guestbook/routes/auth.clj
```
(defn login-page []
  (layout/common
    (form-to [:post "/login"]
      (control text-field :id "screen name")
      (control password-field :pass "Password")
      (submit-button "login"))))
```

To sum up, we can create rules for any fields we'd like to validate. Each rule will use a test to determine whether the field is valid. If any of the fields fail validation, then an error is generated and displayed to the user via the on-error helper.

We can do this because validation errors are associated with the request. Since the function responsible for rendering the page is called within the scope of the same request, it will have access to the errors.

Adding Security

lib-noir also provides a simple way to hash and validate passwords using noir.util.crypt. This namespace provides two functions, encrypt and compare. The first encrypts and salts the password, and the second compares the raw password to the hash string generated by the first. We use the popular jBCrypt library to do the actual encryption.[21]

The signature for the compare function looks like this:

```
(compare raw encrypted)
```

The encrypt function allows specifying the salt, and generates one if none is provided.

```
(encrypt salt raw)
(encrypt raw)
```

We salt passwords to prevent rainbow-table attacks.[22] A rainbow table is effectively a dictionary containing precalculated hashes along with many common passwords used to generate them. Such a table is optimized to make hash lookups efficient, and allows the attacker to easily discover the original password string given its hash. The salt constitutes a randomly generated string that is concatenated with the hashed password. The final hash that's generated is no longer susceptible to such an attack.

Again, we need to require this namespace to our auth namespace to use it.

```
(ns guestbook.routes.auth
  (:require ...
            [noir.util.crypt :as crypt])
```

Until now, we've been sticking user records in our session. Let's implement the functionality to persist the user details when a user registers on our site. We first need to create a user table and write a function to add users to and retrieve users from our database in the db namespace.

---

21. http://www.mindrot.org/projects/jBCrypt/

22. http://en.wikipedia.org/wiki/Rainbow_table

```
guestbook-with-auth/src/guestbook/models/db.clj
(defn create-user-table []
  (sql/with-connection
    db
    (sql/create-table
      :users
      [:id "varchar(20) PRIMARY KEY"]
      [:pass "varchar(100)"])))

(defn add-user-record [user]
  (sql/with-connection db
    (sql/insert-record :users user)))

(defn get-user [id]
  (sql/with-connection db
    (sql/with-query-results
      res ["select * from users where id = ?" id] (first res))))
```

Once that's done, we can reload our db namespace so that the new functions become available, and run (create-user-table) at the REPL console.

We can now navigate back to our auth namespace and write the handle-registration function. Note that we'll also have to require the db namespace in our declaration.

```
(ns guestbook.routes.auth
  (:require ... [guestbook.models.db :as db]))
```

```
guestbook-with-auth/src/guestbook/routes/auth.clj
(defn handle-registration [id pass pass1]
  (rule (= pass pass1)
        [:pass "password was not retyped correctly"])
  (if (errors? :pass)
    (registration-page)
    (do
      (db/add-user-record {:id id :pass (crypt/encrypt pass)})
      (redirect "/login"))))
```

We'll update the POST /register route to use this function when called.

```
(POST "/register" [id pass pass1]
      (handle-registration id pass pass1))
```

When a user attempts to log in subsequently, we'll check his credentials in our login function.

```
guestbook-with-auth/src/guestbook/routes/auth.clj
(defn handle-login [id pass]
  (let [user (db/get-user id)]
    (rule (has-value? id)
          [:id "screen name is required"])
```

```
(rule (has-value? pass)
     [:pass "password is required"])
(rule (and user (crypt/compare pass (:pass user)))
     [:pass "invalid password"])
(if (errors? :id :pass)
(login-page)
(do
  (session/put! :user id)
  (redirect "/")))))
```

We do that by using the crypt/compare function to compare the supplied password to the hashed version we created during the registration.

Specifying MIME Types

In some cases we may wish to specify our data's content type, such as plain text, JSON, and so on. We can do this easily by wrapping the response in the content-type function found in the noir.response namespace.

```
(GET "/records" []
  (noir.response/content-type "text/plain" "some plain text"))
```

Helpers for serving JSON and XML can also be found in noir.response. For JSON responses, the data structure will be automatically converted into a JSON string.

```
(GET "/get-message" []
  (noir.response/json {:message "everything went better than expected!"))
```

This response helper is very useful when dealing with Ajax requests from the client.

Noir API Overview

lib-noir provides even more useful features than we've discussed up to this point.

The cookies namespace provides functions for storing and retrieving cookies. The io namespace contains functions for accessing static resources and handing file uploads. The cache namespace provides facilities for basic content caching. The middleware namespace provides several helpers for creating common types of application handlers and wrappers. Finally, the route namespace provides a function for creating restricted routes. This can be useful for restricting access to pages, as we'll discuss in Chapter 5, *Picture Gallery*, on page 81.

What You've Learned

In this chapter we looked at how the Clojure web stack is structured and at some of the commonly used libraries. We covered the interaction between Ring, Compojure, and lib-noir by seeing the interplay between these libraries when accomplishing tasks such as input validation and session management.

Hopefully, you're now comfortable reading and understanding the code in the guestbook project we created in Chapter 1, *Getting Your Feet Wet*, on page 1. If this isn't the case, I urge you to reread this chapter and try the examples yourself using the REPL environment we set up. Finally, if you haven't already done so, take this opportunity to integrate the examples from this chapter into your guestbook application.

In the next chapter, we'll look at building REST services using the Liberator library.

CHAPTER 3

Liberator Services

In the last chapter we talked about how to write a typical web application and how its components interact with one another. For example, we now know how to manage the routes, write HTML templates, and use sessions for state management. In this chapter we'll look at a different approach to writing applications.

As you've probably noticed, the separation between the client and the server portions of the application is not enforced. If we're not careful we could easily end up with a tightly coupled client and server components. This could become a problem if we wish to add a different client later on—for example, if we decided to create a native mobile version of our application.

In this chapter we'll cover how to use the Liberator library to ensure the separation of concerns between the server and the client.[1] Liberator is a Clojure library for writing RESTful services modeled after webmachine,[2] a popular service framework for Erlang. Its primary feature is that it puts a strong emphasis on decoupling the front end from the back end of your application.

Conceptually, Liberator provides a clean way to reason about your service operations. Each request passes through a series of conditions and handlers defined in the resource. These map to the codes specified by the HTTP RFC 2616, such as 200 - OK, 201 - created, 404 - not found, and so on.

This approach makes it very easy to write standards-compliant services and to group the operations logically. It also means that your services will automatically use the appropriate HTTP codes associated with a particular response.

---

1. http://clojure-liberator.github.io/liberator/
2. https://github.com/basho/webmachine

Due to its focus on the separation of the front-end and back-end logic, Liberator is a natural choice for writing many types of web applications. These include general-purpose services, single-page applications, and applications that might have nonweb clients, such as mobile applications.

Creating the Project

In this section we'll cover how to create a simple application that serves static resources, provides basic session management, and handles JavaScript Object Notation (JSON) operations.

First let's create a new application called *liberator-service* using the *compojure-app* template.

```
lein new compojure-app liberator-service
```

Once the application is created, add Liberator and Cheshire dependencies to our project.clj dependencies vector:[3]

```
:dependencies
[ ...
  [liberator "0.10.0"]
  [cheshire "5.2.0"]]
```

Cheshire is a fast and easy-to-use JSON parsing library. We'll use it for parsing the requests from the client and generating the responses.

At this point, we should be able to start up the read-evaluate-print loop (REPL) by running the start-server in the liberator-service.repl namespace.

Currently, the application displays the default home route created by the template. Let's look at how we can render a Liberator route instead.

Defining Resources

Liberator uses the concept of resources to interact with the client. The resources are simply Ring-compliant handlers that can be used inside your Compojure routes. These resources are defined using the resource and defresource macros. Let's open the liberator-service.routes.home namespace. We'll remove the reference to layout and add the references for resource and defresource to the declaration:

liberator-snippets/home.clj
```
(ns liberator-service.routes.home
  (:require [compojure.core :refer :all]
            [liberator.core
             :refer [defresource resource request-method-in]]))
```

---

3.   https://github.com/dakrone/cheshire

Now we can replace our "/" route with a resource as follows:

```
liberator-snippets/home.clj
(defroutes home-routes
  (ANY "/" request
       (resource
          :handle-ok "Hello World!"
          :etag "fixed-etag"
          :available-media-types ["text/plain"]))))
```

If we reload the page we'll see *Hello World!* displayed. Note that we're using ANY Compojure route for our resource. This allows the Liberator resource to handle the request type.

Say we want to name the resource handler; we can use defresource instead:

```
liberator-snippets/home.clj
(defresource home
  :handle-ok "Hello World!"
  :etag "fixed-etag"
  :available-media-types ["text/plain"])

(defroutes home-routes
  (ANY "/" request home))
```

The request in the preceding route is simply a map that's described in *What's in the Request Map*, on page 27.

A set of keys defined by the Liberator application programming interface represents each resource. Specific actions are in turn associated with each key. A key can fall into one of four categories:

- Decision
- Handler
- Action
- Declaration

Each key can be associated with either constants or functions. The functions should accept a single parameter that is the current context, and return a variety of responses.

The context parameter contains a map with keys for the *request*, the *resource*, and optionally the *representation*. The *request* key points to the Ring request. The *resource* represents the current state of the resource, and the *representation* contains the results of content negotiation.

Let's take a close look at each of the categories and their purposes.

Making Decisions

The decisions are used to figure out how to handle the client request. The decision keys end with a question mark (?) and their handler must evaluate to a Boolean value.

A decision function can return a Boolean value indicating the result of the decision, or it can return a map or a vector. In case a map is returned, the decision is assumed to have been evaluated to true and the contents of the map are merged with the response map. In case a vector is returned, it must contain a Boolean indicating the outcome, followed by a map to be merged with the response.

When any decision has a negative outcome, its corresponding HTTP code will be returned to the client. For example, if we wanted to mark as unavailable the route we defined earlier, we could add a decision key called service-available? and associate it with a false value:

liberator-snippets/home.clj
```
(defresource home
  :service-available? false
  :handle-ok "Hello World!"
  :etag "fixed-etag"
  :available-media-types ["text/plain"])
```

If we reload the page we'll see the *503* response type associated with the *Service not available* response.

Alternatively, we could restrict access to the resource by using the method-allowed? decision key along with a decision function.

```
(defresource home
  :method-allowed?
  (fn [context]
    (= :get (get-in context [:request :request-method]))))
  :handle-ok "Hello World!"
  :etag "fixed-etag"
  :available-media-types ["text/plain"])
```

Since checking the request method is a common operation, Liberator provides a key called :allowed-methods. This key should point to a vector of keywords representing the HTTP methods.

```
(defresource home
  :allowed-methods [:get]
  :handle-ok "Hello World!"
  :etag "fixed-etag"
  :available-media-types ["text/plain"])
```

We can also combine multiple decision functions in the same resource, as seen here:

```
liberator-snippets/home.clj
(defresource home
  :service-available? true

  :method-allowed? (request-method-in :get)

  :handle-method-not-allowed
  (fn [context]
    (str (get-in context [:request :request-method]) " is not allowed"))

  :handle-ok "Hello World!"
  :etag "fixed-etag"
  :available-media-types ["text/plain"])
```

Creating Handlers

A handler function should return a standard Ring response. Handler keys start with the handle- prefix. We saw a handler function when we used the handle-ok key to return the response in our resource.

There are other handlers, such as handle-method-not-allowed and handle-not-found. The full list of handlers can be found on the official documentation page.[4] These handlers can be used in conjunction with the decisions to return a specific response for a particular decision outcome.

For example, if we wanted to return a specific response when the service is not available, we could do the following:

```
liberator-snippets/home.clj
(defresource home
  :service-available? false
  :handle-service-not-available
  "service is currently unavailable..."

  :method-allowed? (request-method-in :get)
  :handle-method-not-allowed
  (fn [context]
    (str (get-in context [:request :request-method]) " is not allowed"))

  :handle-ok "Hello World!"
  :etag "fixed-etag"
  :available-media-types ["text/plain"])
```

Our resource now has custom handlers for each decision outcome.

---

4. http://clojure-liberator.github.io/liberator/doc/handlers.html

Taking Actions

An action represents an update of the current state by the client, such as a PUT, POST, or DELETE request. The action keys end with an exclamation point (!) to indicate that they're mutating the application's internal state.

Once an action occurs, we can return the result to the client using the handle-created handler.

Writing Declaration

Declarations are used to indicate the resource's capabilities. For example, our resource uses the available-media-types declaration to specify that it returns a response of type text/plain. Another declaration we saw is the etag, allowing the client to cache the resource.

Putting It All Together

Let's look at an example of a service that has a couple of resources that allow the client to read and store some data.

The application will display a list of users and allow the client to add additional users to the list. The client will be implemented in JavaScript and use Ajax to communicate with the service.

To start, let's create a static *HTML* page in our public directory and call it home.html. The page contents will look like this:

```
liberator-snippets/home.html
<html>
  <head>
    <title>Liberator Example</title>
    <script type="text/javascript"
            src="//ajax.googleapis.com/ajax/libs/jquery/1.9.0/jquery.min.js">
    </script>

    <script type="text/javascript">
      function renderUsers(users) {
        $('#user-list').empty();
        for(user in users)
          $('#user-list').append($('<li/>', {html: users[user]}));
      }
      function getUsers() {
        $.get("/users", renderUsers);
      }
      function addUser() {
        $.post("/add-user", {user: $('#name').val()}, renderUsers);
      }
```

```
        $(function() {getUsers();});
    </script>
  </head>

  <body>
    <h1>Current Users</h1>

    <ul id="user-list"></ul>
    <input type="text" id="name" placeholder="user name"/>
    <button onclick="addUser()">Add User</button>
  </body>

</html>
```

The page contains functions to render a list of users from given a JSON array, get the current users from the /users URI, and add a new user via the /add-user URI. In addition we have a user-list placeholder for displaying the users, and a text field along with the Add User button for adding new users. The page should look like the following image.

We'll now create corresponding resources to handle each of the operations. To serve the data as JSON we'll first have to add a reference to cheshire.core/generate-string in the declaration of our home namespace:

```
(ns liberator-service.routes.home
  (:require ...
            [cheshire.core :refer [generate-string]]))
```

Next we'll create an atom to hold the list of users:

```
(def users (atom ["John" "Jane"]))
```

The first resource will respond to GET requests and return the contents of the users atom as JSON.

liberator-service/src/liberator_service/routes/home.clj

```
(defresource get-users
  :allowed-methods [:get]
  :handle-ok (fn [_] (generate-string @users))
  :available-media-types ["application/json"])
```

In the resource, we use the :allowed-methods key to restrict it to only serve GET requests. We use the available-media-types declaration to specify that the response is of type application/json. The resource will generate a JSON string from our current list of users when called.

The second resource will respond to POST and add the user contained in the form-params to the list of users. It will then return the new list:

liberator-snippets/home.clj

```
(defresource add-user
  :method-allowed? (request-method-in :post)
  :post!
  (fn [context]
    (let [params (get-in context [:request :form-params])]
      (swap! users conj (get params "user"))))
  :handle-created (fn [_] (generate-string @users))
  :available-media-types ["application/json"])
```

Here we check that the method is POST, and use the post! action to update the existing list of users. We then use the handle-created handler to return the new list of users to the client.

Note that with the resource just detailed, the handle-created value *must* be a function.

The following resource will compile without errors. However, when it runs you'll see the old value of users. This is because (generate-string @users) is evaluated *before* the decision graph is run.

liberator-snippets/home.clj

```
(defresource add-user
  :method-allowed? (request-method-in :post)
  :post!
  (fn [context]
    (let [params (get-in context [:request :form-params])]
      (swap! users conj (get params "user"))))
  :handle-created (generate-string @users)
  :available-media-types ["application/json"])
```

It is therefore important to ensure that you provide the :handle-created key with a function that will be run when the decision graph is executed, as we did in the original example.

You'll notice that nothing is preventing us from adding a blank user. Let's add a check in our service to validate the request to add a new user:

```
liberator-service/src/liberator_service/routes/home.clj
(defresource add-user
  :allowed-methods [:post]
  :malformed? (fn [context]
                (let [params (get-in context [:request :form-params])]
                  (empty? (get params "user"))))
  :handle-malformed "user name cannot be empty!"
  :post!
  (fn [context]
    (let [params (get-in context [:request :form-params])]
      (swap! users conj (get params "user"))))
  :handle-created (fn [_] (generate-string @users))
  :available-media-types ["application/json"])
```

Now, if the value of the user parameter is empty, we'll be routed to handle-mal-formed, which will inform the client that the user name cannot be empty. Next time we try to add an empty user, we'll see a 400 error in the browser:

```
POST http://localhost:3000/add-user 400 (Bad Request)
```

We can now update our page to handle the error and display the message, as follows:

```
liberator-snippets/home1.html
<html>
  <head>
    <meta http-equiv="Content-Type" content="text/html; charset=US-ASCII">
    <title>Liberator Example</title>

    <script type="text/javascript"
            src="//ajax.googleapis.com/ajax/libs/jquery/1.9.0/jquery.min.js">
    </script>

    <script type="text/javascript">
        function renderUsers(users) {
          $('#user-list').empty();
          for(user in users)
            $('#user-list').append($('<li/>', {html: users[user]}));
        }

        function getUsers() {
          $.get("/users", renderUsers);
        }

        function handleError(xhr) {
          $('#error').text(xhr.statusText + ": " + xhr.responseText);
        }
```

```
      function addUser() {
        var jqxhr = $.post("/add-user", {user: $('#name').val()}, renderUsers)
                        .fail(handleError);
      }

      $(function() {getUsers();});
    </script>
  </head>
  <body>
    <h1>Current Users</h1>
    <p id="error"></p>
    <ul id="user-list"></ul>
    <input type="text" id="name" placeholder="user name"/>
    <button onclick="addUser()">Add User</button>
  </body>
</html>
```

Now, if we click the Add User button without filling in the user name field we'll see the following error:

As a final touch, let's add a home resource that will serve our home.html file. To do that we'll add the lib-noir dependency to our project.clj:

```
:dependencies [... [lib-noir "0.7.2"]]
```

Next we'll add references to noir.io and clojure.java.io to the home namespace declaration:

```
(ns liberator-service.routes.home
  (:require [...
            [noir.io :as io]
            [clojure.java.io :refer [file]]))
```

Now we can create a new resource called home that will serve the home.html file:

```
liberator-service/src/liberator_service/routes/home.clj
(defresource home
    :available-media-types ["text/html"]

    :exists?
    (fn [context]
      [(io/get-resource "/home.html")
       {::file (file (str (io/resource-path) "/home.html"))}])

    :handle-ok
    (fn [{{{resource :resource} :route-params} :request}]
      (clojure.java.io/input-stream (io/get-resource "/home.html")))
    :last-modified
    (fn [{{{resource :resource} :route-params} :request}]
      (.lastModified (file (str (io/resource-path) "/home.html")))))
```

The resource will check whether the file exists and when it was last modified. If the file isn't available then io/get-resource will return a nil and the client will get a 404 error. If the file wasn't changed since the last request, the client will be returned a 304 code instead of the file, indicating that it wasn't modified.

Thanks to this check, the file will be served only if it exists and we made changes to it since it was last requested. We can now add a route to serve home.html as our default resource:

```
(ANY "/" request home)
```

Our home namespace containing the service counterparts to the page should look like this:

```
liberator-service/src/liberator_service/routes/home.clj
(ns liberator-service.routes.home
  (:require [compojure.core :refer :all]
            [liberator.core :refer [defresource resource]]
            [cheshire.core :refer [generate-string]]
            [noir.io :as io]
            [clojure.java.io :refer [file]]))
(defresource home
    :available-media-types ["text/html"]

    :exists?
    (fn [context]
      [(io/get-resource "/home.html")
       {::file (file (str (io/resource-path) "/home.html"))}])

    :handle-ok
    (fn [{{{resource :resource} :route-params} :request}]
      (clojure.java.io/input-stream (io/get-resource "/home.html")))
    :last-modified
```

```
    (fn [{{{resource :resource} :route-params} :request}]
      (.lastModified (file (str (io/resource-path) "/home.html")))))

(def users (atom ["foo" "bar"]))
(defresource get-users
  :allowed-methods [:get]
  :handle-ok (fn [_] (generate-string @users))
  :available-media-types ["application/json"])

(defresource add-user
  :allowed-methods [:post]
  :malformed? (fn [context]
                (let [params (get-in context [:request :form-params])]
                  (empty? (get params "user"))))
  :handle-malformed "user name cannot be empty!"
  :post!
  (fn [context]
    (let [params (get-in context [:request :form-params])]
      (swap! users conj (get params "user"))))
  :handle-created (fn [_] (generate-string @users))
  :available-media-types ["application/json"])

(defroutes home-routes
  (ANY "/" request home)
  (ANY "/add-user" request add-user)
  (ANY "/users" request get-users))
```

As you can see, Liberator ensures separation of concerns by design. With the Liberator model you will have small self-contained functions, each of which handles a specific task.

What You've Learned

So far we've been focusing on the server-client-interaction portion of the application. In the next chapter we'll take a deeper look at connecting to and working with databases.

CHAPTER 4

Database Access

In the previous chapters we've primarily focused on handling the interaction between the client and the server, and only skimmed over the topic of persisting our data. In this chapter, we'll cover how to work with relational databases using the clojure.java.jdbc library. We'll then discuss how to write a simple application to generate a PDF report from database records.

Working with Relational Databases

By virtue of running on the Java Virtual Machine, Clojure has access to any database that can be accessed via Java Database Connectivity (JDBC).[1] With it, we can easily access a large number of RDBMS databases, such as MySQL, SQL Server, PostgreSQL, and Oracle. Several libraries are available for working with these databases. Let's take a quick look at our options.

The simplest library for dealing with relational databases is clojure.data.jdbc. When using this library you will have to write custom SQL for each type of database you intend to use. If you know you're going to be using a particular database, such as MySQL or PostgreSQL, this will likely not be a problem for you. However, if you ever decide to migrate, be prepared to modify your queries to match the syntax of your new database.

Another approach for dealing with RDBMS is to use a higher-level library such as SQL Korma (http://sqlkorma.com/). This library will let you write your queries using a Clojure domain-specific language (DSL) and generate the SQL statements targeting the specified back end. The obvious advantage here is that you no longer have to write SQL by hand. However, you will have to learn the DSL and will be limited to accessing only the databases it supports. Later in the book we'll see an example of using it.

---

1.   http://en.wikipedia.org/wiki/Java_Database_Connectivity

For now, we'll focus on using the clojure.data.jdbc library, as it provides all the functionality we need without any additional complexity. We'll use Post-greSQL as our database engine throughout this book.

If you choose to use a different database engine, be aware that there might be slight syntactic differences in your SQL queries.

Accessing the Database

To access the database, we first need to include the necessary libraries in our project.clj file. We need to reference the java.jdbc library as well as the driver for the database we'll be accessing. In case of PostgreSQL we'll require the following dependencies:

```
[org.clojure/java.jdbc "0.2.3"]
[postgresql/postgresql "9.1-901.jdbc4"]
```

With that in place, we can create a new namespace to serve as the model for the application. This namespace is conventionally called models.db. We first have to reference the clojure.data.jdbc library the same way we did in the examples in Chapter 1, *Getting Your Feet Wet*, on page 1.

```
(:require [clojure.java.jdbc :as sql])
```

Next we need to define our database connection. We can do this in several ways. Let's look at these options and their pros and cons.

Defining a Parameter Map

The simplest way to define a connection is by providing a map of connection parameters.

```
(def db {:subprotocol "postgresql"
         :subname "//localhost/my_website"
         :user "admin"
         :password "admin"})
```

This is a common approach; its downside is that the connection information is stored directly in the source. The parameters you're able to supply are also more limited than they would be if you were using the driver directly.

Specifying the Driver Directly

Another option is to provide a JDBC data source and configure it manually. This option is useful if you wish to specify any driver-specific parameters not accessible through the idiomatic parameter map configuration.

```
(def db
  {:datasource
    (doto (PGPoolingDataSource.)
      (.setServerName    "localhost")
      (.setDatabaseName "my_website")
      (.setUser          "admin")
      (.setPassword      "admin")
      (.setMaxConnections 10))})
```

Defining a JNDI String

Finally, we can define the connection by specifying the Java Naming and Directory Interface (JNDI) name for a connection managed by the application server.

```
(def db {:name "jdbc/myDatasource"})
```

Here we've provided the JNDI name as a string. The actual connection will be configured on the application server you're using, and must be given the same name as the one defined in the application. When the application runs, it will query the server for the actual connection details using the name supplied.

This option separates the code in the application from the environment, which is nice. For example, you might have separate development, staging, and production servers. You can point the JNDI connection in each one to its respective database, and when you deploy your application it will pick up the connection details from the environment. The application code does not need to change, and you don't need to remember to keep track of separate profiles or environment configurations when building it.

Now that we have a database connection, let's look at how to accomplish some common tasks with it. Each database operation must be wrapped using the with-connection macro. This macro ensures that the connection is cleaned up before the function exits.

Creating Tables

We create tables by calling the create-table function and providing it the table name, followed by the columns and their types. Let's write a function to create a table to store user records, where each record has an ID and a password.

```
(defn create-users-table []
  (sql/with-connection db
    (sql/create-table
      :users
      [:id "varchar(32) PRIMARY KEY"]
      [:pass "varchar(100)"])))
```

Here, create-table is called to create a new users table. The macro takes a keyword specifying the table name, followed by vectors representing the columns. Each column has the format of [:name type], where name is the name of the column and the type can either be a SQL string or a keyword such as :int, :boolean, or :timestamp. Note: the name of the column cannot have dashes because those are not valid SQL syntax.

Selecting Records

To select records from our database we use the with-query-results macro. It accepts a vector containing the SQL string followed by its arguments and returns a result as a lazy sequence. This allows us to work with the returned data without having to load the entire result into memory.

Because the result is lazy, we must make sure we evaluate it if we intend to return it from the function. If we don't, with-connection will close our connection when we leave the function and the result will be nil. We can use doall to force the evaluation of the entire result. However, if we simply select an element as seen in the following code, that will cause the result to be evaluated implicitly.

```
(defn get-user [id]
  (sql/with-connection db
    (sql/with-query-results
      res ["select * from users where id = ?" id] (first res))))
```

In that code, we've created a function that accepts the user ID parameters and returns the first item from the result set.

Note that we're using a parameterized query by specifying a vector containing the prepared statement string followed by its parameters. This approach is commonly used to prevent SQL injection attacks.

Inserting Records

There are a number of options for inserting records into the database. If you have a map whose keys match the names of the columns in the table, then you can simply use the insert-record function.

```
(defn add-user [user]
  (sql/with-connection db
    (sql/insert-record :users user)))

(add-user {:id "foo" :pass "bar"})
```

If you want to insert multiple records simultaneously, you can use the insert-records function instead.

```
(sql/with-connection db
  (sql/insert-records
    :users
    {:id "foo" :pass "x"}
    {:id "bar" :pass "y"}))
```

We can also use the insert-rows function to specify the records given the values.

```
(defn add-user [id pass]
  (sql/with-connection db
    (sql/insert-rows :users
      [id pass])))
```

The function expects a vector containing the values for each of the columns defined in the table. In case we only want to insert a partial row, we can use insert-values instead.

```
(sql/insert-values :users [:id] ["foo"])
```

The first parameter is the table name. It is followed by a vector specifying the names of the columns to be updated. Lastly, we have another vector containing the values for the columns.

Updating Existing Records

To update an existing record, you can use the update-values and update-or-insert-values functions. The first will require the record to exist in the database, and the second will attempt to update the record and insert a new one if necessary.

```
(sql/update-values
    :users
    ["id=?" "foo"]
    {:pass "bar"})
```

```
(sql/update-or-insert-values
  :users
  ["id=?" "foo"]
  {:pass "bar"})
```

Deleting Records

To delete records from the database, we can use the delete-rows function:

```
(sql/delete-rows :users ["id=?" "foo"])
```

Transactions

We use transactions when we want to run multiple statements and ensure that the statements will be executed only if all of them can be run successfully.

If any of the statements throw an exception, then the transaction will be rolled back to the state prior to running any of the statements.

```
(sql/with-connection db
    (sql/transaction
      (sql/update-values
        :users
        ["id=?" "foo"]
        {:pass "bar"})

      (sql/update-values
        :users
        ["id=?" "bar"]
        {:pass "baz"})))
```

Report Generation

In this section we'll cover how we can easily generate reports from the data we collect in our database using the clj-pdf library.[2] Then we'll discuss how to serve the generated PDF to the browser using the appropriate response type.

Our application will have an employee table that will be populated with some sample data. We'll use this data to create a couple of different PDF reports and allow the users to select the type of report they wish to view.

The first thing we'll need to do is configure our database. For this example we'll be using the PostgreSQL database.

Setting Up the PostgreSQL Database

Installing PostgreSQL is very easy. If you're using OS X, then you can simply run Postgres.app.[3] On Linux, you can install PostgreSQL from your package manager. For example, if you're using Ubuntu you can run sudo apt-get install postgresql.

Once installed, we set the password for the user postgres using the psql shell. The shell can be invoked by running the psql command from the console.

```
sudo -u postgres psql postgres
\password postgres
```

With the default user set up we'll create an admin user with the password set to admin.

```
CREATE USER admin WITH PASSWORD 'admin';
```

---

2.   https://github.com/yogthos/clj-pdf
3.   http://postgresapp.com/

Then we can create a schema called REPORTING to store our reports by running the following command:

```
CREATE DATABASE REPORTING OWNER admin;
```

Note that we're using the admin user here to save time. You should always create a dedicated user and grant only the necessary privileges for any database you wish to run in production.

With the database configuration out of the way, let's create a new application called *reporting-example* using the compojure-app template.

We'll now open the project.clj file and add the necessary dependencies to it:

```
:dependencies [...
               [postgresql/postgresql "9.1-901.jdbc4"]
               [org.clojure/java.jdbc "0.2.3"]
               [clj-pdf "1.11.6"]]
```

Let's start the read-evaluate-print loop (REPL) by running (start-server) in the reporting-example.repl namespace.

With the REPL running, let's create a new namespace called reporting-example.models.db and add our database configuration there.

We'll navigate to the db namespace and create our database connection using clojure.java.jdbc.

reporting-example/src/reporting_example/models/db.clj
```
(ns reporting-example.models.db
  (:require [clojure.java.jdbc :as sql]))


(def db {:subprotocol "postgresql"
         :subname "//localhost/reporting"
         :user "admin"
         :password "admin"})
```

Then we'll make an employee table and populate it with the sample data:

reporting-example/src/reporting_example/models/db.clj
```
(defn create-employee-table []
  (sql/create-table
    :employee
    [:name "varchar(50)"]
    [:occupation "varchar(50)"]
    [:place "varchar(50)"]
    [:country "varchar(50)"]))

(sql/with-connection
  db
  (create-employee-table)
```

```
(sql/insert-rows
  :employee
  ["Albert Einstein", "Engineer", "Ulm", "Germany"]
  ["Alfred Hitchcock", "Movie Director", "London", "UK"]
  ["Wernher Von Braun", "Rocket Scientist", "Wyrzysk", "Poland"]
  ["Sigmund Freud", "Neurologist", "Pribor", "Czech Republic"]
  ["Mahatma Gandhi", "Lawyer", "Gujarat", "India"]
  ["Sachin Tendulkar", "Cricket Player", "Mumbai", "India"]
  ["Michael Schumacher", "F1 Racer", "Cologne", "Germany"]))
```

Finally, we'll write a function to read the records from the table:

reporting-example/src/reporting_example/models/db.clj
```
(defn read-employees []
  (sql/with-connection db
    (sql/with-query-results rs ["select * from employee"] (doall rs))))
```

Let's run read-employees to make sure everything is working as expected. We should see something like the following:

```
(read-employees)

({:country "Germany",
  :place "Ulm",
  :occupation "Engineer",
  :name "Albert Einstein"}
 {:country "UK",
  :place "London",
  :occupation "Movie Director",
  :name "Alfred Hitchcock"}
 ...)
```

You'll notice that the result of calling read-employees is simply a list of maps where the keys are the names of the columns in the table.

Let's see how we can use this to create a table listing the employees in our database.

Report Generation

The clj-pdf library uses syntax similar to Hiccup's to define the elements in the document. The document itself is represented by a vector. The document vector must contain a map representing the metadata as its first element. The metadata is followed by one or more elements representing the document's content.

Let's create a namespace called reporting-example.reports and look at a few examples of creating PDF documents. We'll use the pdf function to create the reports, and the template function to format the input data.

```
(ns reporting-example.reports
  (:require [clj-pdf.core :refer [pdf template]]))
```

The pdf function accepts two arguments. The first can be either a vector representing the document or an input stream from which the elements will be read. The second can be a string representing the output file name or an output stream.

Let's generate our first PDF by running the following in our reports namespace:

```
(pdf
  [{:header "Wow that was easy"}
   [:list
    [:chunk {:style :bold} "a bold item"]
    "another item"
    "yet another item"]
   [:paragraph "I'm a paragraph!"]]
  "doc.pdf")
```

As you can see, the report consists of vectors, each starting with a keyword identifying the type of element, followed by optional metadata and the content. In the preceding report we have a list that contains three rows, followed by a paragraph. The PDF will be written to a file called doc.pdf in our project's root. The contents of the file should look like the following figure.

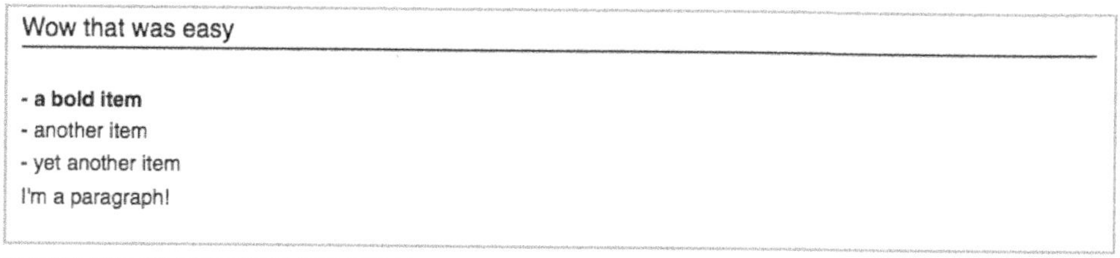
Wow that was easy

- a bold item
- another item
- yet another item

I'm a paragraph!

Figure 13—Our first PDF

Next, let's see how we can use the template macro to format the employee data into a nice table. This macro uses $ to create anchors to be populated from the data using the keys of the same name.

The template returns a function that accepts a sequence of maps and applies the supplied template to each element in the sequence. In our case, since we're building a table, the template is simply a vector with the names of the keys for each cell in the row. We'll add the following template to the reporting-example.reports namespace.

```
(def employee-template
  (template [$name $occupation $place $country]))
```

Let's add the reference to our db namespace and try running our template against the database:

```
reporting-example/src/reporting_example/reports.clj
(ns reporting-example.reports
  (:require [clj-pdf.core :refer [pdf template]]
            [reporting-example.models.db :as db]))
```

We should see the following output after running (employee-template (take 2 (db/read-employees))) in the REPL:

```
(["Albert Einstein" "Engineer" "Ulm" "Germany"]
 ["Alfred Hitchcock", "Movie Director", "London", "UK"])
```

Looks like our template works as expected. Let's use it to generate a report containing the full list of our employees:

```
(pdf
 [{:header "Employee List"}
  (into [:table
         {:border false
          :cell-border false
          :header [{:color [0 150 150]} "Name" "Occupation" "Place" "Country"]}]
        (employee-template (db/read-employees)))]
 "report.pdf")
```

The resulting report should look like the following figure.

Employee List			
Name	Occupation	Place	Country
Albert Einstein	Engineer	Ulm	Germany
Alfred Hitchcock	Movie Director	London	UK
Wernher Von Braun	Rocket Scientist	Wyrzysk	Poland
Sigmund Freud	Neurologist	Pribor	Czech Republic
Mahatma Gandhi	Lawyer	Gujarat	India
Sachin Tendulkar	Cricket Player	Mumbai	India
Michael Schumacher	F1 Racer	Cologne	Germany

Figure 14—Employee table report

Of course, the template we used for this report is boring. Let's look at another example. Here we'll output the data in a list and style each element:

reporting-example/src/reporting_example/reports.clj
```
(def employee-template-paragraph
  (template
    [:paragraph
     [:heading {:style {:size 15}} $name]
     [:chunk {:style :bold} "occupation: "] $occupation "\n"
     [:chunk {:style :bold} "place: "] $place "\n"
     [:chunk {:style :bold} "country: "] $country
     [:spacer]]))
```

Now let's create a report using the employee-template-paragraph by running the following:

```
(pdf
  [{}
   [:heading {:size 10} "Employees"]
   [:line]
   [:spacer]
   (employee-template-paragraph (db/read-employees))]
  "report.pdf")
```

Our new report will look like the following figure.

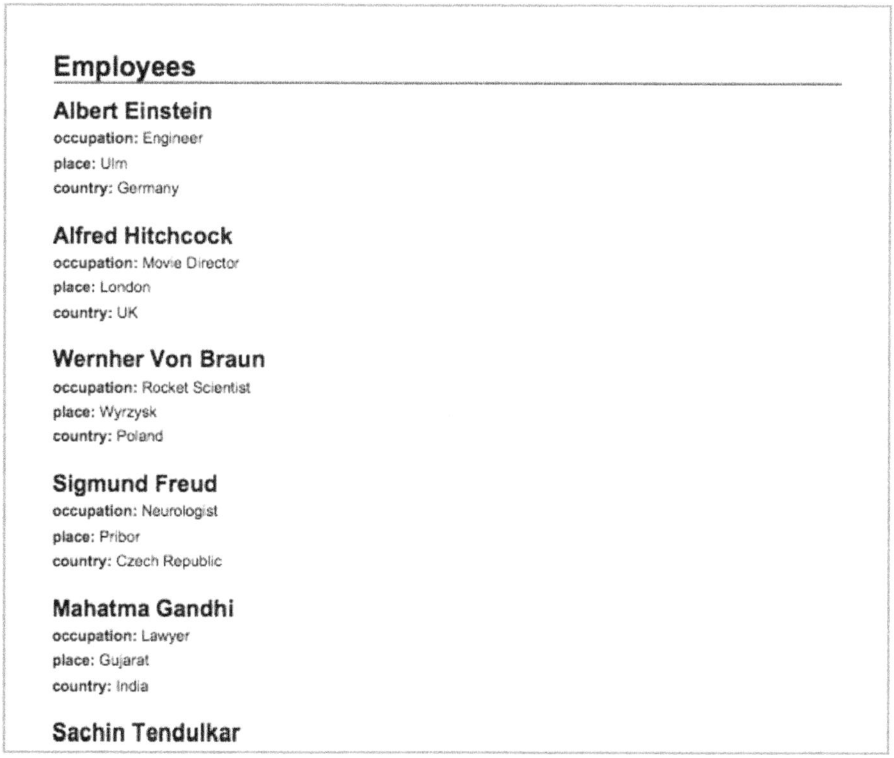

Figure 15—Employee list report

Displaying the Reports

Now that we've created a couple of reports on our data, let's see how we can
serve them from our application. We'll write the functions to create a list and
table reports using the preceding examples:

```
reporting-example/src/reporting_example/reports.clj
(defn table-report [out]
  (pdf
    [{:header "Employee List"}
     (into [:table
            {:border false
             :cell-border false
             :header [{:color [0 150 150]} "Name" "Occupation" "Place" "Country"]}]
           (employee-template (db/read-employees)))]
    out))


(defn list-report [out]
  (pdf
    [{}
     [:heading {:size 10} "Employees"]
     [:line]
     [:spacer]
    (employee-template-paragraph (db/read-employees))]
    out))
```

Next, we'll navigate to reporting-example.routes.home and add some references
needed to generate the report route.

```
reporting-example/src/reporting_example/routes/home.clj
(ns reporting-example.routes.home
  (:require [hiccup.element :refer [link-to]]
            [ring.util.response :as response]
            [compojure.core :refer [defroutes GET]]
            [reporting-example.reports :as reports]
            [reporting-example.views.layout :as layout]))
```

We'll update the home function to provide links to each of the reports:

```
reporting-example/src/reporting_example/routes/home.clj
(defn home []
  (layout/common
    [:h1 "Select a report:"]

    [:ul
     [:li (link-to "/list" "List report")]
     [:li (link-to "/table" "Table report")]]))
```

Now we'll write a function to generate the response. We'll create an input
stream using a supplied byte array and set it as the response. We'll also set

the appropriate headers for the content type, the content disposition, and the length of the content.

reporting-example/src/reporting_example/routes/home.clj
```
(defn write-response [report-bytes]
  (with-open [in (java.io.ByteArrayInputStream. report-bytes)]
    (-> (response/response in)

        (response/header "Content-Disposition" "filename=document.pdf")
        (response/header "Content-Length" (count report-bytes))
        (response/content-type "application/pdf")) ))
```

We'll write another function to generate the report. This function will create a ByteArrayOutputStream that will be used to store the report. Then it will call one of our report-generation functions with it. Once the report is generated we'll call write-response with the contents of the output stream.

reporting-example/src/reporting_example/routes/home.clj
```
(defn generate-report [report-type]
  (try
    (let [out (new java.io.ByteArrayOutputStream)]
      (condp = (keyword report-type)
        :table (reports/table-report out)
        :list  (reports/list-report out))
      (write-response (.toByteArray out)))

    (catch Exception ex
      {:status 500
       :headers {"Content-Type" "text/html"}
       :body (layout/common
               [:h2 "An error has occured while generating the report"]
               [:p (.getMessage ex)])})))
```

Last but not least, we're going to create a new route to serve our reports.

reporting-example/src/reporting_example/routes/home.clj
```
(defroutes home-routes
  (GET "/" [] (home))
  (GET "/:report-type" [report-type] (generate-report report-type)))
```

You should now be able to navigate to http://localhost:3000 and select a link to one of the reports. When you click on the link the corresponding report will be served.

What You've Learned

This covers the basics of working with relational databases. You've now learned how to do the basic database operations and seen a simple reporting application in action. As we've covered in this chapter, database records are easily mapped to Clojure data structures. Therefore, the Clojure community sees object-relational mapping libraries as unnecessary.

In the next chapter we'll put together all the skills you've learned so far to write a picture-gallery application.

CHAPTER 5

Picture Gallery

In this chapter we'll tie together all the concepts you've learned thus far by building a picture-gallery application.

The Development Process

We'll build our application by creating a brief outline of the features to work from, then filling in the details as we go along.

We'll be developing our application interactively using the read-evaluate-print loop (REPL). This will allow us to grow the application without the need for restarts to see new functionality.

Don't be afraid to try things out when using the REPL. For example, if you're writing a particular function to pull some data from the database, try it right in the editor and see its output before hooking it up to the page.

What's in a Gallery

We'll identify the different use cases for our site and then stub out some pages around those. Let's go over a list of actions we'd like our site's users to be able to perform. Each of these use cases will constitute a particular workflow that we can complete independent of others.

Task A: Account Registration

For a user to put content on the site, she needs to have an account. To facilitate this we need a page to collect some user details such as an ID and a password, validate those, and create a database entry for the user.

Task B: Login and Logout

Once a user creates an account, he should be able to log in using the credentials provided. We need to display a login form on our pages if there is no user in the session. If the user logs in successfully, we want to display a logout button instead.

Task C: Uploading Pictures

With the preliminaries out of the way, we can focus on adding some core functionality. First, we need to provide a way for users to upload content to the site. When a picture is uploaded we need to create a thumbnail to display when listing the galleries.

Task D: Displaying Pictures

Now that we can upload pictures, we need to display them. We'll display the thumbnails and use them as links to the full-sized pictures. Since our site is a multiuser one, we also need a way to list user galleries. This way visitors will be able to browse the content from all users.

Task E: Deleting Pictures

Users might wish to remove some of their uploads, and we'll provide an interface to do so. When a user chooses to delete some pictures, he'll need a way to select them and then delete both the pictures and their thumbnails.

Task F: Account Deletion

A user may also wish to remove her account; hopefully this scenario never comes up, but we'll facilitate it just in case. When an account is deleted, we'll have to remove the user from our database and remove all the pictures and thumbnails for that user.

Code Architecture

Now that we've identified what we'd like our site to do, we can begin thinking about how to implement it. To keep things manageable we'll create separate namespaces for each of our workflows. Grouping all the related actions in the same namespace allows us to compartmentalize the logic.

The first step toward understanding the nature of our application is to consider its data model. Figuring out what data we wish to collect and how it will be used will help us understand the workflow and our use cases. Therefore, setting up our database and creating the necessary tables will be the first step of building our application.

If you've worked with a web framework in an object-oriented language, you're probably used to creating an object model and then mapping that model to the database, either by writing SQL statements by hand or using an object-relational mapping framework such as Hibernate to do that for you.[1]

In our application the database will be our data model. Because the logic is kept separate from the data in Clojure, there's no value in copying the maps returned from the database to different data structures. Following this rationale, we'll use our table definitions as the data model for the application. In a later chapter we'll cover how we can use a native Clojure domain-specific language to access the database instead.

Creating the Application

To create the application we'll open Eclipse and then select a new Leiningen project. We'll set the project name to picture-gallery and change our profile from default to compojure-app. If needed, please refer to Chapter 1, *Getting Your Feet Wet*, on page 1, for more details on how to complete this step. We'll use PostgreSQL as our database, so we'll need to add the necessary dependencies to our project. Once your project has been initialized, open the project.clj and add the postgresql, clojure.java.jdbc, and lib-noir dependencies.

picture-gallery-a/project.clj
```
[postgresql/postgresql "9.1-901.jdbc4"]
[org.clojure/java.jdbc "0.2.3"]
[lib-noir "0.7.6"]
```

Since we're using lib-noir, we have to add its middleware to our handler for it to work correctly. We'll open the picture-gallery.handler namespace and add a few things to it. First we have to reference the libraries we'll be using. We'll do this by adding them to the :require section of our namespace definition, at the top.

```
(:require ... [noir.util.middleware :as noir-middleware])
```

We'll use the app-handler middleware found in the noir.middleware namespace to set up the handler for our site. The app-handler will set up all the common middleware, such as session management, for us.

Let's replace the current app definition with the following one.

```
(def app (noir-middleware/app-handler [home-routes app-routes]))
```

We can now remove some of the references from our namespace, since they're provided by the app-handler. Our namespace declaration should now look like the following.

---

1.   http://www.hibernate.org/

```
(ns picture-gallery.handler
  (:require [compojure.route :as route]
            [compojure.core :refer [defroutes]]
            [noir.util.middleware :as noir-middleware]
            [picture-gallery.routes.home :refer [home-routes]]]))
```

With our handler set up, let's navigate to the picture-gallery.repl namespace in the package explorer and run it. This should start up a REPL where you can run the start-server function to start the application. You should see the following output in the REPL after running (start-server).

```
;; Clojure 1.5.1
=> (start-server)
picture-gallery is starting
Started server on port 3000
You can view the site at http://localhost:3000
```

Once the application starts, a new browser window will open, pointing to localhost:3000 and showing a stock template home page like the one in the following figure.

Figure 16—Default page

Application Data Model

We're now ready to start working on creating the application we outlined earlier. Since defining the data model is a prerequisite for all the following tasks, we'll tackle it first.

Configuring the Database

Let's create a new schema called gallery in the database. In PostgreSQL, create an admin user with the password set to admin, then run the following command to add the schema for our application.

```
CREATE DATABASE GALLERY OWNER admin;
```

Now that our database is ready to use, let's look at how to connect to it. We can use clojure.java.jdbc to set up the Java Database Connectivity connection.

We'll create a db namespace under models and set up our database connection there. For simplicity, let's use the first method of defining the database connection that we discussed in Chapter 4, *Database Access*, on page 67. With this method we specify the connection parameters in a map using the format specified by the clojure.java.jdbc library.

picture-gallery-a/src/picture_gallery/models/db.clj
```
(ns picture-gallery.models.db
  (:require [clojure.java.jdbc :as sql]))


(def db
  {:subprotocol "postgresql"
   :subname "//localhost/gallery"
   :user "admin"
   :password "admin"})
```

Defining the Data Model

With the connection set up, we can now look at defining the necessary tables. Let's create a new namespace called picture-gallery.models.schema. This namespace will hold our table definitions and act as documentation for our model.

picture-gallery-a/src/picture_gallery/models/schema.clj
```
(ns picture-gallery.models.schema
  (:require [picture-gallery.models.db :refer :all]
            [clojure.java.jdbc :as sql]))
```

Our first task will be to implement user registration. As our first step, we should try to identify the model for storing the user information.

We'll write a function to create a new table to hold the user accounts. This table will define the user record that we'll use throughout our application.

Each user will need to have an ID and a password. Both of these variables can be strings. Since the password will be hashed, we should make this field long enough to contain it.

Since the user ID represents a unique user, we should make it a primary key. This will prevent users with duplicate IDs from being created.

picture-gallery-a/src/picture_gallery/models/schema.clj
```
(defn create-users-table []
  (sql/with-connection db
    (sql/create-table
      :users
      [:id "varchar(32) PRIMARY KEY"]
      [:pass "varchar(100)"])))
```

Let's run the create-users-table function in the REPL to create the table. You should see the following output if the table was created successfully:

```
#<Namespace gallery.models.schema>
(0)
```

With our users table in place, we're ready to move on to our first task of showing a registration page and providing a way to create user accounts.

Task A: Account Registration

User registration and authentication is a self-contained workflow that is unrelated to the rest of the our application's functionality. This makes it a good candidate for creating a namespace to hold all the authentication functions and routes. We'll create a picture-gallery.routes.auth namespace and, inside it, implement the functions to handle this task.

Before we continue we need to understand the workflow involved in user registration. The user has to enter some identifying information in a form. The form submission has to be processed by the handler to decide whether a user account should be created.

Since all the user data can be collected in a single step, we need a single page with a form to collect the input. The page will call the handler to validate the input and create the user.

As our first step, let's reference the relevant libraries in the namespace declaration.

```
(ns picture-gallery.routes.auth
  (:require [hiccup.form :refer :all]
            [compojure.core :refer :all]
            [picture-gallery.routes.home :refer :all]
            [picture-gallery.views.layout :as layout]
            [noir.session :as session]
            [noir.response :as resp]))
```

The next step will be very similar to what we did with our guestbook application in Chapter 2, *Clojure Web Stack*, on page 25. Registering users consists of collecting the user information we wish to store and creating a record in the database. In our case, we'll simply collect the user ID, a password, and a retyped password to ensure it was entered correctly. Let's create the form and a controller stub for the registration.

We'll start by defining the routes for authentication; the GET route will render the page, and its POST counterpart will handle the submission from the form.

```
picture-gallery-a/src/picture_gallery/routes/auth.clj
(defroutes auth-routes
  (GET "/register" []
       (registration-page))

  (POST "/register" [id pass pass1]
        (handle-registration id pass pass1)))
```

With the routes in place we can write the actual functions to render the page and handle the registration. As you recall, we've already defined our user table and added the id and pass fields to it. We should use the same names for these fields in our form.

```
(defn registration-page [& [id]]
  (layout/common
    (form-to [:post "/register"]
             (label "user-id" "user id")
             (text-field "id" id)
             [:br]
             (label "pass" "password")
             (password-field "pass")
             [:br]
             (label "pass1" "retype password")
             (password-field "pass1")
             [:br]
             (submit-button "create account"))))

(defn handle-registration [id pass pass1]
  (session/put! :user id)
  (resp/redirect "/"))
```

Now that we've defined our routes and written the handler functions, we need to expose these in our handler. To do that we need to add a reference to picture-gallery.routes.auth in the picture-gallery.handler namespace, and update the app definition to include our new routes.

```
(:require ...
          [picture-gallery.routes.auth :refer [auth-routes]])

(def app (noir-middleware/app-handler
           [auth-routes
            home-routes
            app-routes]))
```

We should now be able to browse to localhost:3000/register and see our registration page (which Figure 17, *Registration page*, on page 88 shows).

Note that occasionally the REPL may get into a bad state. This is often triggered when there's an error in the code and a namespace fails to compile. In

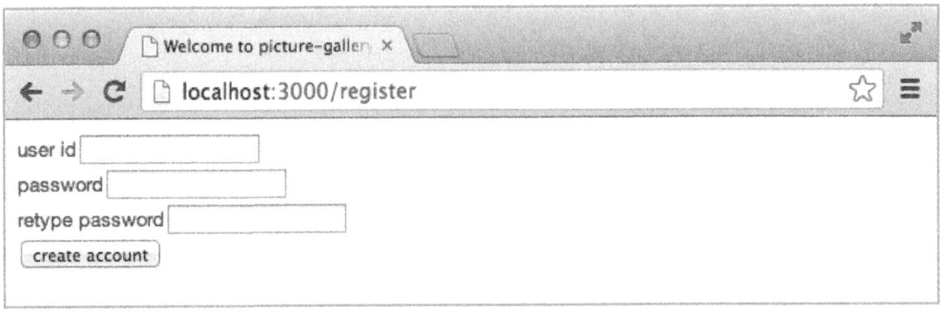

Figure 17—Registration page

this scenario a stale version of the code may be running. If you believe this to be the case, then simply restart the REPL. This will force all the namespaces to be recompiled, and if there were any errors you'll be able to see them in the stack trace that will be displayed in the console.

When the page loads we can check that we're able to submit the user details to the server. We'll now modify the home function in the picture-gallery.routes.home namespace to provide our own content instead of the stock template page.

For starters, if a user is available in the session, let's print the user ID in the greeting. To do that we'll need to reference the noir.session namespace.

```
(ns picture-gallery.routes.home
  (:require ... [noir.session :as session]))
```

Then we'll simply grab the value for the :user key from the session and display it on our page.

```
(defn home []
  (layout/common [:h1 "Hello " (session/get :user)]))
```

Now let's navigate to the localhost:3000/register URL, fill in the user details, and press the Create Account button. We should be taken to the home page and the user ID should be displayed in our welcome message, as in Figure 18, *Home page*, on page 89.

Now that we have our basic registration workflow functioning, we can add some validation to it. We should check that the user didn't forget to provide an ID and that the entered passwords match.

We'll open the picture-gallery.routes.auth namespace and add some validation to the registration form. To do that we'll have to require noir.validation in the namespace declaration.

```
(:require ... [noir.validation :as vali])
```

Figure 18—Home page

Next, we can add the validation function and the error-item formatter the same
way we did in Chapter 2, *Clojure Web Stack*, on page 25.

picture-gallery-a/src/picture_gallery/routes/auth.clj
```
(defn valid? [id pass pass1]
  (vali/rule (vali/has-value? id)
             [:id "user id is required"])
  (vali/rule (vali/min-length? pass 5)
             [:pass "password must be at least 5 characters"])
  (vali/rule (= pass pass1)
             [:pass "entered passwords do not match"])
  (not (vali/errors? :id :pass :pass1)))

(defn error-item [[error]]
  [:div.error error])
```

Now we can update our registration page to validate the input and respond
accordingly.

```
(defn registration-page [& [id]]
  (layout/common
    (form-to [:post "/register"]
             (vali/on-error :id error-item)
             (label "user-id" "user id")
             (text-field "id" id)
             [:br]
             (vali/on-error :pass error-item)
             (label "pass" "password")
             (password-field "pass")
             [:br]
             (vali/on-error :pass1 error-item)
             (label "pass1" "retype password")
             (password-field "pass1")
             [:br]
             (submit-button "create account"))))
```

We'll now update our controller to validate the input and either add the user
to the session and redirect to the home page if validation passes, or render

the registration page. The error will be set by our valid? function and the page will display it using the on-error helper.

```
(defn handle-registration [id pass pass1]
  (if (valid? id pass pass1)
    (do (session/put! :user id)
      (resp/redirect "/"))
    (registration-page id)))
```

Let's try to submit an incomplete registration form to test that our validation rules are now being checked (see the following figure).

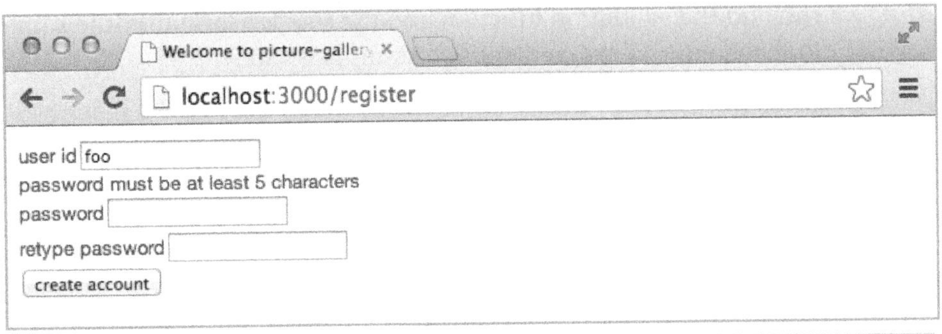

Figure 19—Registration-page error

We can also add a bit of styling to the page to make it look more presentable. To do that we'll open the screen.css file generated by the template. The file is located in the resources/public/css folder. You'll notice that it already has some stock CSS defined. We'll now add our own style to the existing content.

picture-gallery-a/resources/public/css/screen.css
```
body {
    background-color: #fff;
    color: #555;
    font-family: 'Helvetica Neue', Helvetica, Arial, sans-serif;
    font-size: 13px;
}
h1 {
    text-align: center;
}
label {
    width:150px;
    float:left;
}
.error {
    color: red;
}
```

Now the forms will be aligned nicely and errors will show up in red. We won't focus much on style at this point since our page elements might change as we add more functionality. Once we have our pages finalized, we'll revisit our application's styling.

Another feature that we'll add to the form is tab indexes on input fields. This way the user can tab through the fields using the keyboard.

```clojure
(defn registration-page [& [id]]
  (layout/common
    (form-to [:post "/register"]
             (vali/on-error :id error-item)
             (label "user-id" "user id")
             (text-field {:tabindex 1} "id" id)
             [:br]
             (vali/on-error :pass error-item)
             (label "pass" "password")
             (password-field {:tabindex 2} "pass")
             [:br]
             (vali/on-error :pass1 error-item)
             (label "pass1" "retype password")
             (password-field {:tabindex 3} "pass1")
             [:br]
             (submit-button {:tabindex 4} "create account"))))
```

That function has a lot of repetition. This is a clear sign that we should refactor it. Let's write a helper function to add all the common elements:

picture-gallery-a/src/picture_gallery/routes/auth.clj
```clojure
(defn control [id label field]
  (list
    (vali/on-error id error-item)
    label field
    [:br]))

(defn registration-page [& [id]]
  (layout/common
    (form-to [:post "/register"]
             (control :id
                      (label "user-id" "user id")
                      (text-field {:tabindex 1} "id" id))
             (control :pass
                      (label "pass" "password")
                      (password-field {:tabindex 2} "pass"))
             (control :pass1
                      (label "pass1" "retype password")
                      (password-field {:tabindex 3} "pass1"))
             (submit-button {:tabindex 4} "create account"))))
```

The form should now look a little cleaner and provide all the functionality one would expect (as we can see in the following figure).

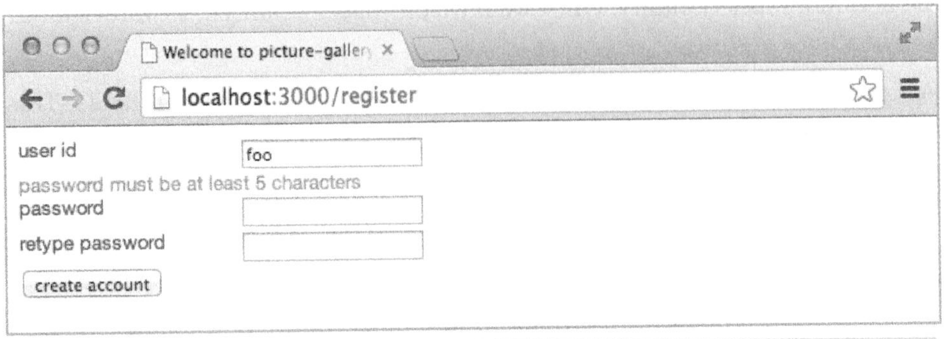

Figure 20—Styled registration page

Note that having less code doesn't always lead to having cleaner code. The code we refactored isn't shorter in the absolute, but each of the functions is clean and easy to read.

It would now be a good idea to provide a link to the registration page so that users can find it. The most logical place to do this would be in the common helper located in the picture-gallery.views.layout namespace. This way all the pages using this layout will display the registration link. Let's open our picture-gallery.views.layout namespace and add a couple of extra library references to its definition.

picture-gallery-a/src/picture_gallery/views/layout.clj
```
(ns picture-gallery.views.layout
  (:require [hiccup.page :refer [html5 include-css]]
            [hiccup.element :refer [link-to]]
            [noir.session :as session]))
```

We'll need noir.session to check if the user exists, and link-to from hiccup.element to provide a link to the registration page. Since we don't want the link to be displayed on the registration page, we'll rename the current version of common to base.

picture-gallery-a/src/picture_gallery/views/layout.clj
```
(defn base [& content]
  (html5
    [:head
     [:title "Welcome to picture-gallery"]
     (include-css "/css/screen.css")]
    [:body content]))
```

Now we can add a new common function that checks if there's a user in the session. If there is, the layout displays the ID; otherwise it shows a link to the registration page.

```
picture-gallery-a/src/picture_gallery/views/layout.clj
(defn common [& content]
  (base
    (if-let [user (session/get :user)]
      [:p user] (link-to "/register" "register"))
    content))
```

Since we don't wish to display the registration link on the /register page, we'll update it to use the base layout instead of common for rendering.

```
picture-gallery-a/src/picture_gallery/routes/auth.clj
(defn registration-page [& [id]]
  (layout/base
    (form-to [:post "/register"]
             (control :id
                      (label "user-id" "user id")
                      (text-field {:tabindex 1} "id" id))
             (control :pass
                      (label "pass" "password")
                      (password-field {:tabindex 2} "pass"))
             (control :pass1
                      (label "pass1" "retype password")
                      (password-field {:tabindex 3} "pass1"))
             (submit-button {:tabindex 4} "create account"))))
```

We can test and see that once we register a user, the ID shows up on the home page when we're directed to it. If we stop and start the server we'll see the registration link instead.

Storing Users in the Database

So far, we've been keeping the user in the session. Now it's time to store the user information in the database instead. We created a users table earlier. All we need to do is to create a function to store the user details in it. Let's open the db namespace again, and add the following code to it:

```
picture-gallery-a/src/picture_gallery/models/db.clj
(defn create-user [user]
  (sql/with-connection
    db
    (sql/insert-record :users user)))
```

There, create-user accepts a map containing two keys. These keys match the column names in the table and the parameters in the form we created. The function simply inserts this record in our users table. In case the record cannot be created, an exception will be thrown.

Let's open the picture-gallery.routes.auth namespace and update it to store the user in the database when an account is created. We'll have to reference picture-gallery.models.db to use the create-user, as well as noir.util.crypt to hash the password before storing it.

```
(:require ...
        [noir.util.crypt :as crypt]
        [picture-gallery.models.db :as db])
```

Then we simply update our controller to call create-user if the login information is valid.

```
(defn handle-registration [id pass pass1]
  (if (valid? id pass pass1)
    (do
      (db/create-user {:id id :pass (crypt/encrypt pass)})
      (session/put! :user id)
      (resp/redirect "/"))
    (registration-page id)))
```

When we try to register a user again, we should see a new user record appear in our users table. We can check that by running the following command from the REPL in the db namespace after registering a user:

```
(sql/with-connection db
  (sql/with-query-results res ["select * from users"] (println res)))

({:id foo,
  :pass $2a$10$YZ/9wi7GFmp1wKWShddqFuLUeSyy2rTIEptw2aI9o96TKu5OLqToy})
```

You might have noticed that our registration page has a small problem. If a user with the same ID already exists in the database, then we get a server error on our page. Not only is this ugly, but it also poses a security risk, as we're exposing the internals of our application to a potential attacker.

Instead, let's catch this exception and display a meaningful message when the user ID is taken. Let's go back to the picture-gallery.routes.auth namespace and make the changes to handle errors and display them.

The page controller will now wrap the call to create-user in a try/catch and render the /register page with an error when an exception is caught instead of redirecting to the home page.

Before that, however, let's make a helper function to check the type of error and make a friendly message instead of the raw exception.

picture-gallery-a/src/picture_gallery/routes/auth.clj

```
(defn format-error [id ex]
  (cond
    (and (instance? org.postgresql.util.PSQLException ex)
      (= 0 (.getErrorCode ex)))
    (str "The user with id " id " already exists!")

    :else
    "An error has occured while processing the request"))

(defn handle-registration [id pass pass1]
  (if (valid? id pass pass1)
    (try
      (db/create-user {:id id :pass (crypt/encrypt pass)})
      (session/put! :user id)
      (resp/redirect "/")
      (catch Exception ex
        (vali/rule false [:id (format-error id ex)])
        (registration-page)))
    (registration-page id)))
```

If you now try to register a user with a duplicate ID, then an error indicating the fact will be displayed in the browser (as we can see here).

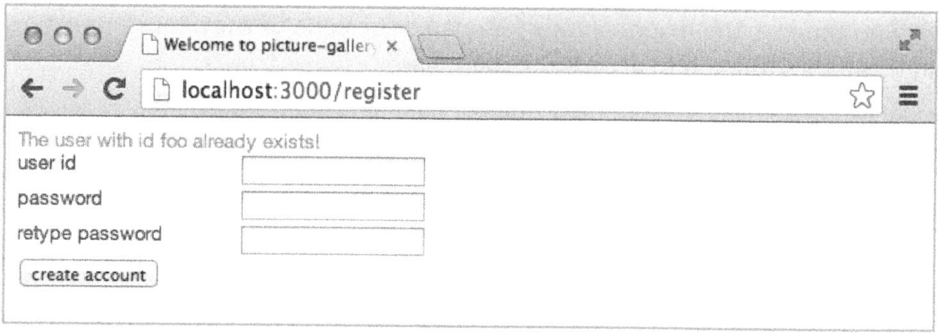

Figure 21—Duplicate-user error

We're now ready to tackle our next task: allowing users to log in and log out after creating an account on our site.

Task B: Login and Logout

Login and logout actions are very simple to implement. To log in the user will submit her ID and password using a login form. These will be checked against the stored credentials, and if they match we'll put the ID in the session.

Let's navigate to our picture-gallery.models.db namespace. We've already added a function to store the users in the database, and we now need to add one to read the users based on the IDs. We'll use the with-query-results macro to get the records and return the first item. If no record matches the supplied ID, we'll simply get a nil value back.

```
(defn get-user [id]
  (sql/with-connection
    db
    (sql/with-query-results
      res ["select * from users where id = ?" id] (first res)))))
```

Note that we have to keep writing (sql/with-connection db ...) for each db statement. Since this gets tedious to do, we'll write a short macro for this task.

picture-gallery-b/src/picture_gallery/models/db.clj
```
(defmacro with-db [f & body]
  `(sql/with-connection ~db (~f ~@body)))

(defn create-user [user]
  (with-db sql/insert-record :users user))

(defn get-user [id]
  (with-db sql/with-query-results
    res ["select * from users where id = ?" id] (first res)))
```

As you can see, the macro simply templates the code to wrap the connection and call the function to access the database.

Now that we have a way to query users, let's add a handler to allow users to log in. The handler will accept the user ID and the password, then compare them to what's stored in the database. We'll put this handler in the picture-gallery.routes.auth namespace:

picture-gallery-b/src/picture_gallery/routes/auth.clj
```
(defn handle-login [id pass]
  (let [user (db/get-user id)]
    (if (and user (crypt/compare pass (:pass user)))
      (session/put! :user id)))

  (resp/redirect "/"))
```

When a user logs out we'll want to clear out that session, so the logout handler will simply call session/clear! to remove any user data that's been accumulated.

```
(defn handle-logout []
  (session/clear!)
  (resp/redirect "/"))
```

Now we'll add the routes for these controllers in our auth-routes definition to expose the functionality to the client.

picture-gallery-b/src/picture_gallery/routes/auth.clj
```clojure
(defroutes auth-routes
  (GET "/register" []
       (registration-page))

  (POST "/register" [id pass pass1]
        (handle-registration id pass pass1))

  (POST "/login" [id pass]
        (handle-login id pass))

  (GET "/logout" []
       (handle-logout)))
```

We'll also need to add the forms to make these handlers accessible from the user interface. Since these forms are common to all pages, the layout is a good candidate for them.

We'll update it to also provide the login and logout links as appropriate. For this we'll have to include hiccup.form in our namespace declaration.

```clojure
(:require ... [hiccup.form :refer :all])
```

With that out of the way, we'll update our common layout to add the login form and a link for the logout route.

picture-gallery-b/src/picture_gallery/views/layout.clj
```clojure
(defn common [& content]
  (base
    (if-let [user (session/get :user)]
      [:div (link-to "/logout" (str "logout " user))]
      [:div (link-to "/register" "register")
       (form-to [:post "/login"]
                (text-field {:placeholder "screen name"} "id")
                (password-field {:placeholder "password"} "pass")
                (submit-button "login"))])
    content))
```

We should now be able to test the login and logout functionality by logging in as a registered user. We've finished implementing all of our authentication tasks. With these out of the way, we'll turn our attention to the next task, which is to allow users to upload their content.

Task C: Uploading Pictures

Since we're creating a new workflow, we should create a new namespace for it. Let's make a picture-gallery.routes.upload namespace for handling this task.

The workflow requires a form to facilitate the upload. Once a file is submitted via this form, we'll need to create a thumbnail to display when listing the user gallery.

The functionality for scaling images can be found in the java.awt.geom package provided by the Java standard library. In this section, we'll use Java interop to wrap it in idiomatic Clojure functions for use in our application.

Let's start by adding all the required references to our namespace. It looks like a lot, but some of them should be familiar. We'll cover how the other ones are used shortly.

picture-gallery-c/src/picture_gallery/routes/upload.clj
```clojure
(ns picture-gallery.routes.upload
  (:require [compojure.core :refer [defroutes GET POST]]
            [hiccup.form :refer :all]
            [hiccup.element :refer [image]]
            [hiccup.util :refer [url-encode]]
            [picture-gallery.views.layout :as layout]
            [noir.io :refer [upload-file resource-path]]
            [noir.session :as session]
            [noir.response :as resp]
            [noir.util.route :refer [restricted]]
            [clojure.java.io :as io]
            [ring.util.response :refer [file-response]]
            [picture-gallery.models.db :as db]
            [picture-gallery.util :refer [galleries gallery-path]])

  (:import [java.io File FileInputStream FileOutputStream]
           [java.awt.image AffineTransformOp BufferedImage]
           java.awt.RenderingHints
           java.awt.geom.AffineTransform
           javax.imageio.ImageIO))
```

Next, we'll create a function to render the upload page, and a handler to process the form's POST action. The page will have a form of type multipart/form-data. The handler will print out the params and render the page. This will let us see what the form submits.

picture-gallery-c/src/picture_gallery/routes/upload.clj
```clojure
(defn upload-page [info]
  (layout/common
    [:h2 "Upload an image"]
    [:p info]
    (form-to {:enctype "multipart/form-data"}
             [:post "/upload"]
             (file-upload :file)
             (submit-button "upload"))))

(defn handle-upload [params]
  (println params)
  (upload-page "success"))
```

As usual, we also have to update our route definitions. We'll have to create the routes and add them to the app declaration in the picture-gallery.handler namespace.

```
(defroutes upload-routes
  (GET "/upload" [info] (upload-page info))

  (POST "/upload" {params :params} (handle-upload params)))
```

In picture-gallery.handler the app declaration should now look as follows:

```
(:require ... [picture-gallery.routes.upload :refer [upload-routes]])
...
(def app (noir-middleware/app-handler
            [auth-routes
             home-routes
             upload-routes
             app-routes]))
```

We can test the form in the browser to see that we're calling the handler successfully. When called, the handler should print the params in the console.

```
{:file
 {:size 15,
  :tempfile #<File /var/folders/mv/sch8x99yc30gp/T/ring-multipart-60387396.tmp>,
  :content-type application/octet-stream,
  :filename cloud.jpg}}
```

We can see that the params have a single key called :file. The :file key points to a map that in turn contains the following keys:

- :tempfile — The file itself
- :filename — The name of the file being uploaded
- :content-type — The content type of the file being uploaded
- :size — The size of the file in bytes

This gives us all the necessary information to save the file. Let's update our handler and the route definition to use the :file parameter and check that a file has been selected:

```
(defn handle-upload [{:keys [filename] :as file}]
  (println file)
  (upload-page
    (if (empty? filename)
      "please select a file to upload"
      "success")))
(defroutes upload-routes
  (GET "/upload" [info] (upload-page info))

  (POST "/upload" [file] (handle-upload file)))
```

All that's left is to save the file to disk. The application's public folder would be an obvious place to store the files. Unfortunately, when we later package our application as a JAR this location will no longer be writable. Instead, we'll create a galleries directory and store the files there.

Let's start by creating a add-gallery-path helper:

```
(defn gallery-path []
  "galleries")
```

We'll use the noir.io/upload-file helper function to handle file uploads. It accepts a path, a map representing the file, and an optional flag signifying whether the path should be created if it doesn't exist.

We'll simply call it from our controller and catch any exceptions that might be thrown if we're unable to save the file. The message from the exception will be set as the info parameter for our page to be displayed to the user. If the upload is successful, we'll display the image we uploaded.

```
(defn handle-upload [{:keys [filename] :as file}]
  (upload-page
    (if (empty? filename)
      "please select a file to upload"

      (try
        (noir.io/upload-file (gallery-path) file :create-path? true)
        (image {:height "150px"}
          (str "/img/" (url-encode filename)))

        (catch Exception ex
          (str "error uploading file " (.getMessage ex)))))))
```

We use url-encode on the file name to ensure that it can be displayed correctly even if it contains special characters that aren't valid in a URL string. To display the image, we have to create a new route and a handler responsible for serving the file we uploaded to the client.

```
(defn serve-file [file-name]
  (file-response (str (gallery-path) File/separator file-name)))

(defroutes upload-routes
  ...
  (GET "/img/:file-name" [file-name] (serve-file file-name)))
```

We can now test that uploading works as expected by going to the upload page and uploading an image. We'll see our image displayed on the page if everything went well. Refer to the following two figures.

Figure 22—Selecting a file to upload

Figure 23—File uploaded successfully

We can now browse to the galleries folder at the root of our project and see that the file was indeed created there.

Generating Thumbnails

Now that we can upload the files, we'll look at how to generate the thumbnail when a file is uploaded. The image needs to be scaled and then stored in a new file. We'll define the size of our thumbnail as 150 pixels, and prefix the thumbnail files with thumb_. Let's make a couple of constants for these values.

```
(def thumb-size 150)
(def thumb-prefix "thumb_")
```

Next, we'll write a function to scale the image. Here we'll leverage the Affine-Transform class provided by the Java standard library to create a scale operation, and use AffineTransformOp to do the transformation. The filter method on the transform-op will use the original image to produce the scaled image we require.

picture-gallery-c/src/picture_gallery/routes/upload.clj
```
(defn scale [img ratio width height]
  (let [scale       (AffineTransform/getScaleInstance
                      (double ratio) (double ratio))

        transform-op (AffineTransformOp.
                       scale AffineTransformOp/TYPE_BILINEAR)]
    (.filter transform-op img (BufferedImage. width height (.getType img)))))
```

Let's test that our scale function works correctly; copy an image file with the name image.jpg into our project's root and run the following from the REPL:

```
(ImageIO/write
  (scale (ImageIO/read (io/input-stream "image.jpg")) 0.5 150 150)
  "jpeg"
  (File. "scaled.jpg"))
```

If the function worked correctly, we should end up with a scaled.jpg in the same folder, with a size of 150 pixels by 150 pixels.

Next we'll read the uploaded file's image data by using the ImageIO class. Once we have an image, we'll grab its width and height, and scale it to the height defined by the thumb-size constant.

picture-gallery-c/src/picture_gallery/routes/upload.clj
```
(defn scale-image [file]
  (let [img        (ImageIO/read file)
        img-width  (.getWidth img)
        img-height (.getHeight img)
        ratio      (/ thumb-size img-height)]
    (scale img ratio (int (* img-width ratio)) thumb-size)))
```

We'll also test scale-image by calling it from the REPL. It's a good idea to test it with a few images with different dimensions to make sure that they all scale correctly.

```
(ImageIO/write
  (scale-image (io/input-stream "image.jpg"))
  "jpeg"
  (File. "scaled.jpg"))
```

All that's left to do is write a function to save the thumbnail and call it after we call upload-file in our controller.

picture-gallery-c/src/picture_gallery/routes/upload.clj
```clojure
(defn save-thumbnail [{:keys [filename]}]
  (let [path (str (gallery-path) File/separator)]
    (ImageIO/write
      (scale-image (io/input-stream (str path filename)))
      "jpeg"
      (File. (str path thumb-prefix filename)))))

(defn save-thumbnail [{:keys [filename]}]
  (let [path (str (gallery-path) File/separator)]
    (ImageIO/write
      (scale-image (io/input-stream (str path filename)))
      "jpeg"
      (File. (str path thumb-prefix filename)))))
```

In our save-thumbnail function, we call resource-path to get the path of our public folder. Then we call ImageIO/write with the output of scale-image to generate the thumbnail file. We can now update the handle-upload function to call save-thumbnail each time a file is uploaded.

```clojure
(defn handle-upload [{:keys [filename] :as file}]
  (upload-page
    (if (empty? filename)
      "please select a file to upload"

      (try
        ;;save the file and create the thumbnail
        (noir.io/upload-file (gallery-path) file :create-path? true)
        (save-thumbnail file)
        ;;display the thumbnail
        (image {:height "150px"}
          (str "/img/" thumb-prefix (url-encode filename)))
        (catch Exception ex
          (str "error uploading file " (.getMessage ex)))))))
```

Now if we upload a file from our upload page we'll see both the file and a thumbnail in our galleries folder.

Saving Files to the User Folder

Since our site has multiple users, each user will have his own gallery. We now need some logic for figuring out a unique gallery path for each user. The simplest approach is to employ the user ID that we collect when a new account is registered, since it's required to be unique.

We'll update the gallery-path function to generate a unique path in the galleries folder based on the user ID that's currently in the session. We should also extract the base path into a separate variable, so it can be used when viewing galleries from other users:

```
(def galleries "galleries")

(defn gallery-path []
  (str galleries File/separator (session/get :user)))
```

Next, let's update the serve-file function and its route to use the user ID when looking up the file:

picture-gallery-c/src/picture_gallery/routes/upload.clj
```
(defn serve-file [user-id file-name]
  (file-response (str galleries File/separator user-id File/separator file-name)))
```

picture-gallery-c/src/picture_gallery/routes/upload.clj
```
(GET "/img/:user-id/:file-name" [user-id file-name]
    (serve-file user-id file-name))
```

Currently, we're checking whether the path exists each time we try to save a file. It would be better to simply ensure that the path is created during the registration. Let's create a new function called create-gallery-path and call it whenever a user account is created.

The function will use gallery-path to get the path string, and java.io.File to create a new folder for the user. We'll have to update our namespace declaration to reference those:

```
(ns picture-gallery.routes.auth
  (:require ...
            [picture-gallery.routes.upload :refer [gallery-path]])
  (:import java.io.File))
```

Then, we'll add the create-gallery-path function and call it in handle-registration to ensure that a new gallery path is created each time a user registers.

picture-gallery-c/src/picture_gallery/routes/auth.clj
```
(defn create-gallery-path []
  (let [user-path (File. (gallery-path))]
    (if-not (.exists user-path) (.mkdirs user-path))
    (str (.getAbsolutePath user-path) File/separator)))
```

picture-gallery-c/src/picture_gallery/routes/auth.clj
```
(defn handle-registration [id pass pass1]
  (if (valid? id pass pass1)
    (try
      (db/create-user {:id id :pass (crypt/encrypt pass)})
      (session/put! :user id)
      (create-gallery-path)
      (resp/redirect "/")
      (catch Exception ex
        (vali/rule false [:id (format-error id ex)])
        (registration-page)))
    (registration-page id)))
```

If we upload a file now, we'll see that both the file and the thumbnail are created under the galleries/<userid> path.

You might have noticed that we have a small problem. The file-upload page doesn't require the user to log in to access it. We should fix this by checking if the user is in the session before displaying the page.

```
(defn upload-page [info]
  (if (session/get :user)
    (layout/common
      [:h2 "Upload an image"]
      [:p info]
      (form-to {:enctype "multipart/form-data"}
               [:post "/upload"]
               (file-upload :file)
               (submit-button "upload")))
    (resp/redirect "/")))
```

With that change we'll be redirected back to the home page when we try to navigate to the upload page in the browser without having logged in.

We've solved this particular instance of the problem. However, we also need to do this for the upload handler and for any other user-specific pages. Writing the if statement every time is tedious and error-prone.

The good news is that lib-noir provides a way to specify rules for restricting access to pages. Let's see how to create a rule to check that the user is present in the session before displaying a page.

We'll navigate to the picture-gallery.handler namespace and create a new function called user-page. This function must accept a single parameter that is the request map. The function can then decide whether the URI should be accessible. In our case, we simply wish to know that a user is present in the session before we allow access to the restricted pages.

```
(ns picture-gallery.handler
  ...
  (:require ... [noir.session :as session]))
```

picture-gallery-c/src/picture_gallery/handler.clj
```
(defn user-page [_]
  (session/get :user))
```

The underscore (_) in the user-page's arguments vector simply indicates that the argument will be ignored.

We now need to update our handler to set the access rules using the :access-rules key. The app-handler will use the noir.util.middleware/wrap-access-rules middleware to apply the rules to restricted pages. In our case, we have a single rule: the user-page function.

picture-gallery-c/src/picture_gallery/handler.clj
```
(def app (noir-middleware/app-handler
            [auth-routes
             home-routes
             upload-routes
             app-routes]
            :access-rules [user-page]))
```

With the access rules in place, we can use the noir.util.route/restricted macro to restrict access to pages. Let's update our upload routes to use this macro.

```
(ns picture-gallery.routes.upload
  (:require ... [noir.util.route :refer [restricted]])
  ...)
```

picture-gallery-c/src/picture_gallery/routes/upload.clj
```
(defroutes upload-routes
  (GET "/img/:user-id/:file-name" [user-id file-name]
       (serve-file user-id file-name))
  (GET "/upload" [info] (restricted (upload-page info)))

  (POST "/upload" [file] (restricted (handle-upload file))))
```

We can now remove the check from our upload page and test that the functionality is still the same.

picture-gallery-c/src/picture_gallery/routes/upload.clj
```
(defn upload-page [info]
    (layout/common
      [:h2 "Upload an image"]
      [:p info]
      (form-to {:enctype "multipart/form-data"}
               [:post "/upload"]
               (file-upload :file)
               (submit-button "upload"))))
```

Using the restricted macro makes the intent more clear than using an if, and it's more flexible in case our restrictions need to be more complex than the one we already set up.

Storing Image Lists in the Database

Since our next tasks are to display images, we'll need to create some metadata for tasks such as looking up all the images belonging to a specific user.

The best place to store such metadata is in the database. We should create a table and use it to store references for each image that gets uploaded.

We'll create a new table called images that will contain a reference to the user ID and image name. Let's open the gallery.models.schema namespace and add a new table definition there.

picture-gallery-c/src/picture_gallery/models/schema.clj
```
(defn create-images-table []
  (sql/with-connection db
    (sql/create-table
      :images
      [:userid "varchar(32)"]
      [:name "varchar(100)"])))
```

We can now evaluate it and run (create-images-table) in the REPL. With the images table in place, we simply need to insert a record each time we upload an image. We'll write a function that does that and put it in our db namespace.

picture-gallery-c/src/picture_gallery/models/db.clj
```
(defn add-image [userid name]
  (with-db
    sql/transaction

    (if (sql/with-query-results
          res
          ["select userid from images where userid = ? and name = ?" userid name]
          (empty? res))

      (sql/insert-record :images {:userid userid :name name})
      (throw
        (Exception. "you have already uploaded an image with the same name")))))
```

In the add-image function, we check to see if the user already uploaded an image with the same name to prevent accidentally overwriting existing images.

All we have to do now is add the db namespace reference in the upload namespace and call the add-image function after we upload each image in our upload page's controller.

```
(ns picture-gallery.routes.upload
  ...
  (:require ... [picture-gallery.models.db :as db]))
```

picture-gallery-c/src/picture_gallery/routes/upload.clj
```
(defn handle-upload [{:keys [filename] :as file}]
  (upload-page
    (if (empty? filename)
      "please select a file to upload"
      (try
        (upload-file (gallery-path) file)
        (save-thumbnail file)
        (db/add-image (session/get :user) filename)
```

```
(image {:height "150px"}
  (str "/img/"
       (session/get :user)
       "/"
       thumb-prefix
       (url-encode filename)))

(catch Exception ex
  (str "error uploading file " (.getMessage ex)))))))))
```

Next time we upload an image, we can check that a new record is created in the database. We've now completed all the functionality needed for users to upload their files.

We should take a moment to do some cleanup before moving on.

Refactoring Common Code

Some of the code we've written will be useful for other pages. For example, when we display our galleries we'll need to know the thumbnail prefix's name and the user gallery's path.

Let's create a picture-gallery.util namespace and move the code for the thumb-prefix, galleries and gallery-path functions there in anticipation of our upcoming tasks. In addition to that we'll create a couple of functions for generating the URI for the image and the thumbnail.

picture-gallery-c/src/picture_gallery/util.clj
```
(ns picture-gallery.util
  (:require [noir.session :as session]
            [hiccup.util :refer [url-encode]])
  (:import java.io.File))

(def thumb-prefix "thumb_")

(def galleries "galleries")

(defn gallery-path []
  (str galleries File/separator (session/get :user)))

(defn image-uri [userid file-name]
  (str "/img/"  userid "/" (url-encode file-name)))

(defn thumb-uri [userid file-name]
  (image-uri userid (str thumb-prefix file-name)))
```

We now have to remember to update the auth and upload namespaces to reference the util namespace.

```
(ns picture-gallery.routes.auth
  (:require ...
            [picture-gallery.util
             :refer [gallery-path]]))

(ns picture-gallery.routes.upload
  (:require ...
            [picture-gallery.util
             :refer [galleries gallery-path thumb-prefix thumb-uri]]))
```

The code for handling the upload can now be cleaned up by using the thumb-uri helper:

picture-gallery-d/src/picture_gallery/routes/upload.clj
```
(defn handle-upload [{:keys [filename] :as file}]
  (upload-page
    (if (empty? filename)
      "please select a file to upload"
      (try
        (upload-file (gallery-path) file)
        (save-thumbnail file)
        (db/add-image (session/get :user) filename)
        (image {:height "150px"}
          (thumb-uri (session/get :user) filename))
        (catch Exception ex
          (str "error uploading file " (.getMessage ex)))))))
```

Now that we have our upload code refactored, we should provide an upload link in our common layout when there is a user in the session.

```
(defn common [& content]
  (base
    (if-let [user (session/get :user)]

      (list
       [:div (link-to "/upload" "upload images")]
       [:div (link-to "/logout" (str "logout " user))])

      [:div (link-to "/register" "register")
       (form-to [:post "/login"]
                (text-field {:placeholder "screen name"} "id")
                (password-field {:placeholder "password"} "pass")
                (submit-button "login"))])

    content))
```

We already have a check to see if a user is in the session and to display the logout button. As we get more pages done, our user menu will continue to grow. This is a sign that we should extract it into a separate function.

picture-gallery-c/src/picture_gallery/views/layout.clj
```
(defn guest-menu []
  [:div (link-to "/register" "register")
   (form-to [:post "/login"]
            (text-field {:placeholder "screen name"} "id")
            (password-field {:placeholder "password"} "pass")
            (submit-button "login"))])

(defn user-menu [user]
  (list
    [:div (link-to "/upload" "upload images")]
    [:div (link-to "/logout" (str "logout " user))]))

(defn common [& content]
  (base
    (if-let [user (session/get :user)]
      (user-menu user)
      (guest-menu))
    content))
```

Let's navigate to our home page and test that everything works as expected following our refactoring efforts. Specifically, we should still be able to browse to the upload page after logging in, and upload files as we did previously.

Task D: Displaying Pictures

We now have all the pieces in place to start displaying the pictures in our gallery. We simply have to load all the thumbnails associated with the user and show them on the page. When clicked, a thumbnail will display the full-size picture.

Since we store references to uploaded images in the database, we can easily write a function to query all images with the given user ID in our db namespace.

picture-gallery-d/src/picture_gallery/models/db.clj
```
(defn images-by-user [userid]
  (with-db
    sql/with-query-results
    res ["select * from images where userid = ?" userid] (doall res)))
```

Let's test that the function does what we intended by running it against a user we registered earlier and see if we get a list of pictures we uploaded as that user.

```
(images-by-user "foo")
```

```
({:name "logo.jpg", :userid "foo"})
```

We can start by displaying the thumbnails on the welcome page when the user logs in. As this is a brand-new workflow, let's create a new namespace called picture-gallery.routes.gallery and add the functions to display the gallery for the user there.

Again, we'll add all the required references to the namespace declaration and see how they're used as we add functionality.

picture-gallery-d/src/picture_gallery/routes/gallery.clj
```clojure
(ns picture-gallery.routes.gallery
  (:require [compojure.core :refer :all]
            [hiccup.element :refer :all]

            [picture-gallery.views.layout :as layout]
            [picture-gallery.util
             :refer [thumb-prefix image-uri thumb-uri]]

            [picture-gallery.models.db :as db]
            [noir.session :as session]))

(defn thumbnail-link [{:keys [userid name]}]
  [:div.thumbnail
   [:a {:href (image-uri userid name)}
    (image (thumb-uri userid name))]])
(defn display-gallery [userid]
  (or
    (not-empty (map thumbnail-link (db/images-by-user userid)))
    [:p "The user " userid " does not have any galleries"]))

(defn gallery-link [{:keys [userid name]}]
  [:div.thumbnail
   [:a {:href (str "/gallery/" userid)}
    (image (thumb-uri userid name))
    userid "'s gallery"]])

(defn show-galleries []
    (map gallery-link (db/get-gallery-previews)))

(defroutes gallery-routes
  (GET "/gallery/:userid" [userid] (layout/common (display-gallery userid))))
```

We'll create two helper functions. The first will generate a div with our thumbnail link and add a thumbnail class to it. The second will read the images for the user in the session and convert them to thumbnails by mapping thumbnail-link across them. If the user doesn't have any images to display, we'll provide a helpful message to indicate that.

picture-gallery-d/src/picture_gallery/routes/gallery.clj
```
(defn thumbnail-link [{:keys [userid name]}]
  [:div.thumbnail
   [:a {:href (image-uri userid name)}
    (image (thumb-uri userid name))]])
(defn display-gallery [userid]
  (or
    (not-empty (map thumbnail-link (db/images-by-user userid)))
    [:p "The user " userid " does not have any galleries"]))
```

We'll also define a new route to display the gallery for a given user ID.

picture-gallery-d/src/picture_gallery/routes/gallery.clj
```
(defroutes gallery-routes
  (GET "/gallery/:userid" [userid] (layout/common (display-gallery userid))))
```

This means we'll need to add a reference to picture-gallery.routes.gallery to our picture-gallery.handler namespace and add the new route to our routes vector.

```
(:require ...
          [picture-gallery.routes.gallery :refer [gallery-routes]])
...
(def app (noir-middleware/app-handler
          [auth-routes
           home-routes
           upload-routes
           gallery-routes
           app-routes]
          :access-rules [user-page]))
```

picture-gallery-d/src/picture_gallery/handler.clj
```
(def app (noir-middleware/app-handler
          [auth-routes
           home-routes
           upload-routes
           gallery-routes
           app-routes]
          :access-rules [user-page]))
```

If we create a user called foo and upload some images, we can then navigate to http://localhost:3000/gallery/foo and see the images we uploaded. We can also test that we get a friendly error if we enter an invalid user ID.

Let's also update our screen.css in the resources/public/css folder to add a bit of style for the thumbnails.

picture-gallery-d/resources/public/css/screen.css
```
.thumbnail {
    float:left;
    padding: 5px;
    margin: 8px;
```

```
    border-style:solid;
    border-width:1px;
    border-color:#ccc;
    box-shadow:             4px 4px 6px -1px #222;
    -moz-box-shadow:        4px 4px 6px -1px #222;
    -webkit-box-shadow: 4px 4px 6px -1px #222;
}
```

All that's left is to display links to galleries on the home page. To do that we'll add another function to our db namespace. This function will pull a single image for each user.

picture-gallery-d/src/picture_gallery/models/db.clj
```
(defn get-gallery-previews []
  (with-db
    sql/with-query-results
    res
    ["select * from
      (select *, row_number() over (partition by userid) as row_number from images)
      as rows where row_number = 1"]
    (doall res)))
```

We'll also add a function in our gallery namespace to generate the gallery links. It's similar to the thumbnail-link function, except that it links to the gallery page instead.

picture-gallery-d/src/picture_gallery/routes/gallery.clj
```
(defn gallery-link [{:keys [userid name]}]
  [:div.thumbnail
   [:a {:href (str "/gallery/" userid)}
    (image (thumb-uri userid name))
    userid "'s gallery"]])
```

We can now create a helper to display all the available galleries by user.

picture-gallery-d/src/picture_gallery/routes/gallery.clj
```
(defn show-galleries []
    (map gallery-link (db/get-gallery-previews)))
```

Finally, we can update our home page to display the available galleries from all the users on our site.

picture-gallery-d/src/picture_gallery/routes/home.clj
```
(ns picture-gallery.routes.home
  (:require [compojure.core :refer :all]
            [picture-gallery.views.layout :as layout]
            [noir.session :as session]
            [picture-gallery.routes.gallery :refer [show-galleries]]))

(defn home []
  (layout/common (show-galleries)))
```

Now that users are able to navigate to different galleries on the site, we need to add a Home button in our menu. We'll take this opportunity to further improve the menu.

picture-gallery-d/src/picture_gallery/views/layout.clj
```
(defn make-menu [& items]
  [:div (for [item items] [:div.menuitem item])])
(defn guest-menu []
  (make-menu
    (link-to "/" "home")
    (link-to "/register" "register")
    (form-to [:post "/login"]
             (text-field {:placeholder "screen name"} "id")
             (password-field {:placeholder "password"} "pass")
             (submit-button "login"))))
(defn user-menu [user]
  (make-menu
    (link-to "/" "home")
    (link-to "/upload" "upload images")
    (link-to "/logout" (str "logout " user))))
```

Each menu item is wrapped in a div with the class of menuitem. We'll add some CSS to style these items so that they flow across the top of the page.

picture-gallery-d/resources/public/css/screen.css
```
.menuitem {
    float: left;
    margin-right: 10px;
}

.content {
    clear: both;
    padding: 20px;
}
```

We've also added a content class to clear the left float after the menu and add some padding to our content. We'll wrap our content in a div with this class.

picture-gallery-d/src/picture_gallery/views/layout.clj
```
(defn common [& content]
  (base
    (if-let [user (session/get :user)]
      (user-menu user)
      (guest-menu))
    [:div.content content]))
```

By this point, we've built a site where users can register accounts, log in, upload pictures, and view the pictures grouped by user. We'll now add the ability for users to delete pictures they have uploaded.

Task E: Deleting Pictures

It's reasonable for users to want to remove images they no longer wish to display. We need to provide a way for users to select images they wish to remove and tell the application about it. To delete a picture, we'll do the following:

- Delete the image
- Delete the thumbnail
- Delete the database entry for the image

Since the images can be removed only by the owner, we'll check if the page matches the user in the session. When this is the case, we'll allow the user to mark pictures he wishes to delete and submit his selection using the Delete button.

So far, we've only been creating static pages. Let's look at how to add some client-side interaction using Ajax. In this section, we'll include JavaScript in our page, call our handler using an HTTP POST from the browser, and return a JavaScript Object Notation response to the client.

We'll use an Ajax call to notify the server of the images to be deleted and update the page to reflect the result of the operation.

First, let's create a function in the picture-gallery.models.db namespace to delete the image from the database.

```
picture-gallery-e/src/picture_gallery/models/db.clj
(defn delete-image [userid name]
  (with-db
    sql/delete-rows :images ["userid=? and name=?" userid name]))
```

Then we'll add a function in the picture-gallery.routes.upload namespace to perform the three deletion tasks we outlined. We need to provide the function with the user ID and the image name to accomplish its task.

We'll wrap the actions in a try/catch block. If the deletion is successful, we'll return ok. If we encounter any errors, we'll return the error message instead.

```
picture-gallery-e/src/picture_gallery/routes/upload.clj
(defn delete-image [userid name]
  (try
    (db/delete-image userid name)
    (io/delete-file (str (gallery-path) File/separator name))
    (io/delete-file (str (gallery-path) File/separator thumb-prefix name))
    "ok"
    (catch Exception ex (.getMessage ex))))
```

Next, we'll add a handler to handle the deletion of multiple images, along with its route.

picture-gallery-e/src/picture_gallery/routes/upload.clj
```
(defn delete-images [names]
  (let [userid (session/get :user)]
    (resp/json
      (for [name names] {:name name :status (delete-image userid name)})))))

(defroutes upload-routes
  (GET "/img/:user-id/:file-name" [user-id file-name]
      (serve-file user-id file-name))

  (GET "/upload" [info] (restricted (upload-page info)))

  (POST "/upload" [file] (restricted (handle-upload file)))

  (POST "/delete" [names] (restricted (delete-images names))))
```

There, delete-images accepts a list of names for the images to be deleted. We then grab the user ID from the session, call delete-image for each image name, and return the outcome of each operation to the client.

Since our plan is to be able to select multiple thumbnails and call the /delete route using Ajax, we need to add some JavaScript to our page. We'll create a new file under resources/public/js called gallery.js. Our gallery page will load this file, which will provide the client-side functions for managing the gallery.

Let's write a function to select some images and make the Ajax call. We'll be using jQuery to help with our JavaScript, so let's include it in our base layout. This necessitates referencing include-js from hiccup.page in the namespace declaration.

```
(:require ...
      [hiccup.page :refer [html5 include-css include-js]])
...

(html5 base [& content]
  [:head
   [:title "Welcome to picture-gallery"]
   (include-css "/css/screen.css")
   (include-js "//code.jquery.com/jquery-2.0.2.min.js")]
  [:body content])
```

We're finally ready to write our function to delete the images on the client side.

```
function deleteImages() {
    var selectedInputs = $("input:checked");
    var selectedIds = [];
```

```
selectedInputs
.each(function() {
        selectedIds.push($(this).attr('id'));
    });
if (selectedIds.length < 1) alert("no images selected");
else
    $.post("/delete",
        {names: selectedIds},
        function(response) {
            var errors = $('<ul>');
            $.each(response, function() {
            if("ok" === this.status) {
                var element = document.getElementById(this.name);
                $(element).parent().parent().remove();
            }
            else
                errors
                .append($('<li>',
                        {html: "failed to remove " +
                                this.name +
                                ": " +
                                this.status}));
            });
            if (errors.length > 0)
                $('#error').empty().append(errors);
        },
        "json");
}
```

In that code, we select checked inputs and then grab the ID attribute for each of them. Next we make an HTTP POST and pass those IDs to our delete-images handler on the server.

The server returns a list of update statuses. When the update is successful, the status is set to ok and we delete the corresponding element. Otherwise, we create an error message based on the status and display it to the user.

The JavaScript file needs to be referenced on the page in order to run. We can do this using the include-js the same way we did with jQuery in our layout. Since the JavaScript is specific to the gallery page, we'll add it directly in the route declaration.

```
(:require ... [hiccup.page :refer :all])
```

picture-gallery-e/src/picture_gallery/routes/gallery.clj
```
(defroutes gallery-routes
  (GET "/gallery/:userid" [userid]
      (layout/common
        (include-js "/js/gallery.js")
        (display-gallery userid))))
```

We'll also require a couple of changes in the way we render our thumbnails, as currently there are no check boxes associated with them for the user to check. Let's add the necessary references to our gallery namespace and update the thumbnail-link as follows:

```
(:require ...
          [hiccup.form :refer [check-box]])
```

picture-gallery-e/src/picture_gallery/routes/gallery.clj
```
(defn thumbnail-link [{:keys [userid name]}]
  [:div.thumbnail
   [:a {:class name :href (image-uri userid name)}
    (image (thumb-uri userid name))
    (if (= userid (session/get :user)) (check-box name))]])
```

Now, if the userid matches the one in the session, we'll also render a check box along with the name of the image in our thumbnail div (see the following figure).

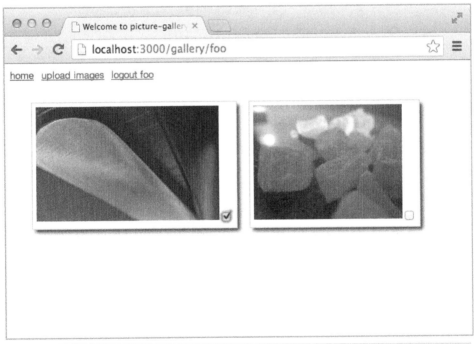

Figure 24—Gallery check box

The check box is there, but we can't interact with it yet. To do that we'll update display-gallery to provide a Delete button and a div to display the errors.

```
picture-gallery-e/src/picture_gallery/routes/gallery.clj
(defn display-gallery [userid]
  (if-let [gallery (not-empty (map thumbnail-link (db/images-by-user userid)))]
    [:div
     [:div#error]
     gallery
     (if (= userid (session/get :user))
       [:input#delete {:type "submit" :value "delete images"}])]
    [:p "The user " userid " does not have any galleries"]))
```

Now, if we have a gallery to display we'll also provide a Delete button when the user is the owner of the gallery. We'll bind the delete function to the button in our gallery.js when the page loads.

```
picture-gallery-e/resources/public/js/gallery.js
$(document).ready(function(){
    $("#delete").click(deleteImages);
});
```

We should now be able to test and see that each thumbnail has a check box when the owner of the gallery views the gallery page. If we select a few images and press the Delete button, they disappear from the page. We can also check that the images and the thumbnails are correctly deleted on disk and in the database.

Ajax and the Servlet Context

The preceding code will work fine when the application runs standalone. However, if we ran our application on an application server, the Ajax request would fail because the full URL would need to have the application context prefixed.

Unfortunately for us, the browser is not aware that our application has a context. One way we can get around this problem is to populate a variable on the page before we serve it.

The request map contains a key with the name :context. The value of this key is exactly what we're looking for. This might appear to be a bit of a conundrum. After all, we don't wish to have to pass the request explicitly to all our handlers just so we can grab the context from it.

Luckily, Compojure uses the compojure.response.Renderable protocol to convert what the handler returns into a Ring response. This protocol looks like this:

```
(defprotocol Renderable
  (render [this request]
    "Render the object into a form suitable for the given request map."))
```

As you can see, the protocol defines a single method called render. This method accepts the object instance and the request that we're after.

To use this protocol, we'll first need to add a reference to it and the ring.util.response/response to our picture-gallery.views.layout namespace declaration:

picture-gallery-e/src/picture_gallery/views/layout.clj
```clojure
(ns picture-gallery.views.layout
  (:require [hiccup.page :refer [html5 include-css]]
            [hiccup.element :refer [link-to]]
            [noir.session :as session]
            [hiccup.form :refer :all]
            [hiccup.page :refer [include-css include-js]]
            [ring.util.response :refer [content-type response]]
            [compojure.response :refer [Renderable]]))
```

Since we're implementing the protocol, we'll need to set the appropriate response headers manually. To do that we'll create the utf-8-response function to set the content type to *text/html* and the encoding to *UTF-8*.

picture-gallery-e/src/picture_gallery/views/layout.clj
```clojure
(defn utf-8-response [html]
  (content-type (response html) "text/html; charset=utf-8"))
```

Next, we'll create a RenderablePage type that will extend the Renderable protocol. We'll move the code from our base layout function to the render method.

Since we now have access to the request, we can add a JavaScript variable to the head section of our page with the value of the context.

Lastly, the body of the render method will have to be wrapped in the response function we included earlier. The final result is as follows:

picture-gallery-e/src/picture_gallery/views/layout.clj
```clojure
(deftype RenderablePage [content]
  Renderable
  (render [this request]
    (utf-8-response
      (html5
        [:head
         [:title "Welcome to picture-gallery"]
         (include-css "/css/screen.css")
         [:script {:type "text/javascript"}
          (str "var context=\"" (:context request) "\";")]
         (include-js "//code.jquery.com/jquery-2.0.2.min.js")]
        [:body content]))))
```

The base layout function will now return an instance of the RenderablePage instead of generating the layout:

picture-gallery-e/src/picture_gallery/views/layout.clj

```
(defn base [& content]
  (RenderablePage. content))
```

Finally, we'll update our JavaScript to prepend the variable to the URL when making the POST request.

picture-gallery-e/resources/public/js/gallery.js

```
$.post(context + "/delete",
      {names: selectedIds},
      function(response) {
         var errors = $('<ul>');
         $.each(response, function() {
         if("ok" === this.status) {
             var element = document.getElementById(this.name);
             $(element).parent().parent().remove();
         }
         else
             errors
             .append($('<li>',
                     {html: "failed to remove " +
                             this.name +
                             ": " +
                             this.status}));
         });
         if (errors.length > 0)
             $('#error').empty().append(errors);
      },
    "json");
```

Now the context will be prepended to the URL. When the context is not available, the variable will contain a blank string and the request will work exactly as it did before.

Task F: Account Deletion

When the user decides to delete her account, we need to delete all the user-related information from the database, as well as all the user's files. Luckily, we already wrote a function to delete individual images and their references. All we have to do is select all images associated with the user and pass them to this function. Then we have to remove the account from the users table and delete the user folder.

The picture-gallery.routes.auth namespace contains the logic related to authentication and user account management. We'll navigate there and add the logic for account deletion by adding the delete-account-page function.

Account deletion will be applicable only to the user in session, obviously, so we need to mark the route as restricted. To do that we have to reference noir.util.route in the namespace declaration.

```
(:require ... [noir.util.route :refer [restricted]])
```

Next, we'll add a route that will delete the account when called.

picture-gallery-f/src/picture_gallery/routes/auth.clj
```
(GET "/delete-account" []
    (restricted (delete-account-page)))
```

When the user chooses to delete the account, we'd like to make sure it's not an accident. The account-deletion page will redirect to a confirmation page to provide an option to back out.

picture-gallery-f/src/picture_gallery/routes/auth.clj
```
(defn delete-account-page []
  (layout/common
    (form-to [:post "/confirm-delete"]
      (submit-button "delete account"))
    (form-to [:get "/"]
      (submit-button "cancel"))))
```

Let's add a route for the account-removal confirmation page.

picture-gallery-f/src/picture_gallery/routes/auth.clj
```
(POST "/confirm-delete" []
      (restricted (handle-confirm-delete)))
```

If the user makes it to the /confirm-delete page, then we know she really wishes to remove the account, and we'll carry out the necessary tasks.

picture-gallery-f/src/picture_gallery/routes/auth.clj
```
(defn handle-confirm-delete []
  (let [user (session/get :user)]
    (doseq [{:keys [name]} (db/images-by-user user)]
      (delete-image user name))
    (clojure.java.io/delete-file (gallery-path))
    (db/delete-user user))
  (session/clear!)
  (resp/redirect "/"))
```

The tasks include calling delete-image from the upload namespace for each image the user uploaded, deleting the user from the users table in the database, and deleting the user's image directory. Once the account data has been deleted, we'll clear the session and redirect the user to the home page.

For this function to work, we'll need to reference picture-gallery.routes.upload in our namespace declaration to use the delete-image function.

```
(:require ... [picture-gallery.routes.upload :refer [delete-image]])
```

Finally, we need to create a delete-user function in our db namespace to delete users from the table.

picture-gallery-f/src/picture_gallery/models/db.clj
```
(defn delete-user [userid]
  (with-db sql/delete-rows :users ["id=?" userid]))
```

Let's test that the preceding works by removing one of the users we added during our testing. If everything worked as expected, we should now add a link in our user-menu to expose this functionality through our user interface.

picture-gallery-f/src/picture_gallery/views/layout.clj
```
(defn user-menu [user]
  (make-menu
    (link-to "/" "home")
    (link-to "/upload" "upload images")
    (link-to "/logout" (str "logout " user))
    (link-to "/delete-account" "delete account")))
```

This concludes the tasks that we outlined at the start of the chapter. We now have a fully functional multiuser picture gallery.

What You've Learned

In this chapter we put together the skills acquired in previous chapters to create our application. In the next chapter we'll add some final touches and get our application ready for deployment.

CHAPTER 6

Finishing Touches

We're now done with all the workflows we set out to create for our application. Although it's functional, it's certainly not visually appealing. Let's look at how we could style our user interface a little better using CSS and JavaScript.

Adding Some Style

As we discussed in Chapter 1, *Getting Your Feet Wet*, on page 1, you shouldn't embed the CSS in your Hiccup templates. Instead, we'll assign the appropriate ID and class tags to the elements we wish to style. Then we can use those in a CSS file to specify the actual styles for the elements.

First, let's set a general style for the body of the page. We'll open the screen.css and set the following style for the body.

picture-gallery-style-tests/resources/public/css/screen.css

```
body {
    margin: 0px;
    background: #C8D9C9;
    color: #525952;
    font-family: 'Helvetica Neue', Helvetica, Arial, sans-serif;
    font-size: 13px;
}
```

We'll set the margin to 0 pixels, add background and text colors, and set the default font for the body of our pages.

Next, let's make our menu look a bit nicer. Here we'll provide an ID to the menu div, called usermenu, and set the class for each menu item to menuitem.

picture-gallery-style-tests/src/picture_gallery/views/layout.clj

```
(defn make-menu [& items]
  [:div#usermenu (for [item items] [:div.menuitem item])])
```

Then we can set the style for the menu tag in CSS so that it spans the whole width of the page and has a shadow on the bottom. We also need to set inline-block for display to ensure that it expands to contain the menu items.

picture-gallery-style-tests/resources/public/css/screen.css
```
#usermenu {
    background-color: #878C87;
    width: 100%;
    border-bottom-color: #dedede;
    line-height: 25px;
    border:1px solid;
    border-color:#ccc;
    -webkit-box-shadow: 0 8px 6px -6px #555;
    -moz-box-shadow: 0 8px 6px -6px #555;
    box-shadow: 0 8px 6px -6px #555;
    margin-bottom: 25px;
    display: inline-block;
}
```

Next, we'll style the menu links to make them stand out more.

picture-gallery-style-tests/resources/public/css/screen.css
```
#usermenu a:link {text-decoration: none; color: white;}
#usermenu a:hover {text-decoration: underline; color: white;}
#usermenu a:visited {text-decoration: none; color: white;}
```

Now let's style the menu items themselves.

picture-gallery-style-tests/resources/public/css/screen.css
```
.menuitem {
    color: #D1F0DA;
    font-size: 15px;
    font-weight:bold;
    float: left;
    list-style: none;
    padding: 5px;
    margin: 5px;
}
```

We can also style our Submit button to look nicer by setting its size and border style.

picture-gallery-style-tests/resources/public/css/screen.css
```
input[type=submit] {
    background: #99A699;
    padding: 5px 8px 5px;
    color: #fff;
    font-weight: bold;
    -moz-border-radius: 5px;
    -webkit-border-radius: 5px;
    -moz-box-shadow: 0 1px 3px #999;
```

```
        -webkit-box-shadow: 0 1px 3px #999;
        text-shadow: 0 -1px 1px #222;
        border-bottom: 1px solid #222;
        cursor: pointer;
}
```

Adding Color with JavaScript

We can add a bit of style to our image thumbnails using JavaScript. We'll use the AlbumColors library (which you can find on GitHub) to find the dominant colors in the image and set the background of the thumbnail div to the most dominant color.[1]

To use the library we'll save it to our resources/public/js folder as colors.js and add a new JavaScript file called site.js for our site. We'll now include these files in our base layout.

picture-gallery-style-tests/src/picture_gallery/views/layout.clj
```
(include-js "//code.jquery.com/jquery-2.0.2.min.js"
            "/js/colors.js"
            "/js/site.js")
```

In site.js, we'll call the AlbumColors library to grab the colors for each thumbnail and style the div accordingly.

picture-gallery-style-tests/resources/public/js/site.js
```
function colorStr(color) {
    return "rgb("+color[0]+","+color[1]+","+color[2]+")";
}
function setColor(div, colors) {
    var bgColor = colors[0];
    var textColor = colors[1];
    div.css("background-color", colorStr(bgColor));
    div.find('a').css("color", colorStr(textColor));
}
$(document).ready(function(){
    $(".thumbnail")
            .each(function() {
              var div = $(this);
              var url = div.find('img').attr('src');
              var thumbColors = new AlbumColors(url);

              var color = "";
              thumbColors.getColors(function(colors) {
              setColor(div, colors);
        });
    });
});
```

---

1. https://github.com/chengyin/albumcolors

When we reload our page with these changes, the background for each thumbnail should be set to its primary color and the font color should be set to the complementary color. The gallery should now look something like the following figure.

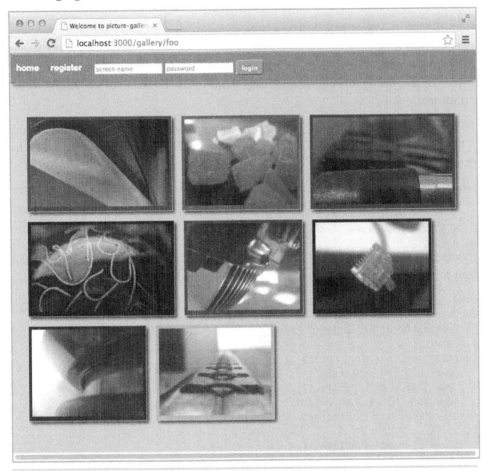

Figure 25—Picture gallery with style applied

Unit Tests

There are many schools of thought on how, what, and when to test. This is a very sensitive subject for many people. As such, I will simply give an overview of the basic tools available for testing and leave it up to you to decide how and when to use them.

The Test API

Clojure provides built-in support for testing via the clojure.test namespace. When a new project is created a test package will be generated along with it.

Let's take a quick look at what this application programming interface (API) looks like and how to work with it. The simplest way to write tests is to create assertions using the is macro. The following are a few examples of how it works:

```
(is (= 4 (+ 2 2)))

(is (= 5 (+ 2 2)))

FAIL in  (:1)
    expected: (= 5 (+ 2 2))
    actual: (not (= 5 4))
false

(is (even? 2))

(is (instance? String 123))
FAIL in (:1)
expected: (instance? String 123)
  actual: java.lang.Long
false
```

As you can see, the is macro can take any expression. If the expression fails, the macro will print the expression along with the actual result, then return false; otherwise it will return true.

We can also group our tests together by using the testing macro. This macro accepts a string name for the group of tests followed by the assertions.

```
(testing "Collections"
  (is (coll? {}))
  (is (coll? #{}))
  (is (coll? []))
  (is (coll? '())))
```

Finally, we can define tests by using the deftest macro:

```
(deftest collections-test
  (testing "Collections"
    (is (coll? {}))
    (is (coll? #{}))
    (is (coll? []))
    (is (coll? '()))))
```

The tests defined using deftest can be called like regular functions. You can also run all the tests in the read-evaluate-print loop (REPL) by calling run-tests. All tests in the application's test folder can be run via Leiningen by calling lein test. The API contains a number of other helpers, as well, but I hope that the preceding examples will prove sufficient for you to get started.

Finally, it's worth mentioning that there are a number of test frameworks for Clojure, such as Midje and Speclj.[2,3] Furthermore, test frameworks are available specifically for testing web applications. The two popular choices to explore are Peridot and Kerodon.[4,5]

These frameworks provide many features not found in the core testing API, and if your testing needs go beyond the basics we explored here, these will make excellent tools in your Clojure toolbox.

Testing the Application

Our application has two types of routes. There are routes that serve the user-interface (UI) portion of the application to be rendered by the browser, and those that expose the handlers for the UI actions. We'll look at writing some tests for our application's login handler.

We already have a test harness defined for our application. You can find it under the test/picture_gallery/test/ directory. The test handler is called handler.clj. If we open it up, we can see that it defines a test called test-app.

This test is currently failing because our application doesn't respond with the result it expects when the / URI is requested. We'll first identify the scenarios that we'd like to test:

- No parameters are supplied during the login.
- The parameters supplied do not match a user in the database.
- The login is successful.

To request a route in our application we can use the following code:

```
(app (request <method> <url> <params>))
```

The response will be a standard Ring response, which was described in Chapter 2, *Clojure Web Stack*, on page 25.

---

2.   https://github.com/marick/Midje
3.   http://speclj.com/
4.   https://github.com/xeqi/peridot
5.   https://github.com/xeqi/kerodon

We'd like to call the /login URL and pass it the user ID and the password. However, we only wish to test the request handler and not the model. Our test shouldn't depend on what users are currently populated in the database.

Unfortunately, the handle-login function in the picture-gallery.routes.auth namespace calls the get-user from the picture-gallery.models.db namespace. When we call it from our tests we'll be querying the actual users in our database.

In some languages it's possible to use monkey patching to get around this problem. This approach allows you to simply redefine the offending function at runtime with your own version. The downside of this approach is that the change is global and therefore might interact poorly with code that expects the original version.

Clojure provides a with-redefs macro that redefines Vars within the scope of its body. This approach gives us the ability to make runtime modifications in a safer fashion, where we know exactly what code is affected.

For our purposes, we'll redefine the get-users function with a mock function for the scope of our tests. It's handy that we didn't have to plan for this when writing our application's business logic. Let's look at how this works in action. We'll first define a mock function that will return a test user.

picture-gallery-style-tests/test/picture_gallery/test/handler.clj
```clojure
(defn mock-get-user [id]
  (if (= id "foo")
    {:id "foo" :pass (encrypt "12345")}))
```

We'll also need to reference noir.util.crypt/encrypt for it to encrypt the password.

picture-gallery-style-tests/test/picture_gallery/test/handler.clj
```clojure
(ns picture-gallery.test.handler
  (:require [clojure.test :refer :all]
            [ring.mock.request :refer :all]
            [noir.util.crypt :refer [encrypt]]
            [picture-gallery.handler :refer :all]))
```

We can now redefine the picture-gallery.models.db/get-user with the mock function before running our test:

```clojure
(with-redefs [picture-gallery.models.db/get-user mock-get-user]
  (app (request :post "/login" {:id "foo" :pass "12345"})))
```

When we run the preceding code in the REPL, we see that a redirect is returned along with a cookie containing our session ID:

```clojure
{:status 302
 :headers {"Set-Cookie" ("ring-session=0645d310-892b-43c0-a4d5-dcaa87859a67;Path=/")
           "Location" "/"}
 :body ""}
```

Now we can test the case for when no user is found:

```
(with-redefs [picture-gallery.models.db/get-user mock-get-user]
  (app (request :post "/login" {:id "bar" :pass "12345"})))
```

This time no session is created and we're simply redirected to the application's / URL:

```
{:status 302
 :headers {"Set-Cookie" ()
           "Location" "/"}
 :body ""}
```

Let's put this all together and write the unit tests for the login portion of our application.

picture-gallery-style-tests/test/picture_gallery/test/handler.clj
```
(ns picture-gallery.test.handler
  (:require [clojure.test :refer :all]
            [ring.mock.request :refer :all]
            [noir.util.crypt :refer [encrypt]]
            [picture-gallery.handler :refer :all]))
(defn mock-get-user [id]
  (if (= id "foo")
    {:id "foo" :pass (encrypt "12345")}))
(deftest test-login
  (testing "login success"
    (with-redefs [picture-gallery.models.db/get-user mock-get-user]
      (is
        (-> (request :post "/login" {:id "foo" :pass "12345"})
          app :headers (get "Set-Cookie") not-empty))))

  (testing "password mismatch"
    (with-redefs [picture-gallery.models.db/get-user mock-get-user]
      (is
        (-> (request :post "/login" {:id "foo" :pass "123456"})
          app :headers (get "Set-Cookie") empty?))))

  (testing "user not found"
    (with-redefs [picture-gallery.models.db/get-user mock-get-user]
      (is
        (-> (request :post "/login" {:id "bar" :pass "12345"})
          app :headers (get "Set-Cookie") empty?)))))
```

Logging

Most real-world applications require some sort of logging functionality. At the very least we want to log any errors that happen in our application. This will allow us to go back and trace the cause of the errors if they happen in production.

Several logging options are available. In this section we'll use the Timbre library.[6] First, we'll need to include it in our project file:

picture-gallery-logging/project.clj
```
[com.taoensso/timbre "2.6.1"]
```

Then we can start using it by requiring it in our namespace and calling the trace info, warn, debug, and fatal functions. Let's add logging to the upload namespace and log errors if an exception occurs when we try to delete a file.

```
(ns picture-gallery.routes.upload
  (:require ...
  [taoensso.timbre
    :refer [trace debug info warn error fatal]]))
```

picture-gallery-logging/src/picture_gallery/routes/upload.clj
```
(defn delete-image [userid name]
  (try
    (db/delete-image userid name)
    (io/delete-file (str (gallery-path) File/separator name))
    (io/delete-file (str (gallery-path) File/separator thumb-prefix name))
    "ok"
    (catch Exception ex
      (error ex "an error has occured while deleting" name)
      (.getMessage ex))))
```

That's all there is to it. To test this, we can upload an image and delete it from the directory outside the application. Then when we go to delete it from the UI, we'll get an exception. This exception will now be logged.

Timbre configuration is specified by a vector containing the keys that represent the path to a particular configuration item. For example, if we wanted to set a custom timestamp pattern in our logs, we could call set-config!.

Let's open the picture-gallery.handler namespace and add a reference to Timbre.

```
(ns picture-gallery.handler
  (:require ... [taoensso.timbre :as timbre]))
```

Then in the init function, we'll initialize the configuration as follows:

```
(timbre/set-config! [:timestamp-pattern] "yyyy-MM-dd HH:mm:ss")
```

We can also use the configuration to redirect the log output to a specific file. By default all the logs will end up in the standard out. However, by providing custom log appenders, we can specify where certain types of logs should go.

---

6.   https://github.com/ptaoussanis/timbre

To specify an appender, we need to add it to the appenders path in the config, as in the following example:

```
(timbre/set-config!
  [:appenders :info-appender]
  {:min-level :info
  :enabled? true
  :async? false
  :max-message-per-msecs 100
  :fn info-appender})
```

The error-appender is just a function that accepts a map containing the following keys: :ap-config, :level, :prefix, :message, and :more. A simple appender function might look like the following:

```
(defn info-appender [{:keys [level message]}]
  (println "level:" level "message:" message))
```

We can now replace the println statements with the appropriate log statements:

```
(defn init []
  (timbre/set-config!
    [:appenders :info-appender]
    {:min-level :info
     :enabled? true
     :async? false
     :max-message-per-msecs 100
     :fn info-appender
     })
  (timbre/info "picture-gallery started successfully"))

(defn destroy []
  (timbre/info "picture-gallery is shutting down"))
```

When the server stars up, we'll see something like the following in the log:

```
2013-May-04 12:31:12 -0400 Helios.local INFO [picture-gallery.handler]
 - picture-gallery started successfully
```

A more realistic example would be to use a readymade appender like rotor. Rotor is a rotating log-file appender provided by the following dependency:

picture-gallery-logging/project.clj
```
[com.postspectacular/rotor "0.1.0"]
```

We can now create a configuration for rotor that's similar to one we made previously:

```
(ns picture-gallery.handler
  (:require ...
    [taoensso.timbre :as timbre]
    [com.postspectacular.rotor :as rotor]))
```

```
picture-gallery-logging/src/picture_gallery/handler.clj
(defn init []
  (timbre/set-config!
    [:appenders :rotor]
    {:min-level :info
     :enabled? true
     :async? false ; should be always false for rotor
     :max-message-per-msecs nil
     :fn rotor/append})

  (timbre/set-config!
    [:shared-appender-config :rotor]
    {:path "error.log" :max-size (* 512 1024) :backlog 10})

  (timbre/info "picture-gallery started successfully"))
```

Note that the rotor appender requires a configuration of its own. We provide it with a path, a maximum size before rotating the log, and the number of old log files to retain:

```
(set-config!
  [:shared-appender-config :rotor]
  {:path "/var/log/error.log" :max-size (* 512 1024) :backlog 10})
```

We now have a sensible log configuration for our application. If we happen to get any errors in production, we'll be able to go back and see what caused them. This will help us find the cause and fix them.

Now that we've built our exciting gallery application, let's look at how we can make it available for consumption. Since we're running on top of the Java Virtual Machine, we have excellent deployment options whether we wish to deploy to a hosting provider, a virtual private server, or a cloud service.

Application Profiles

In many situations you may have to run your application using different configurations. For example, your application might depend on a set of variables such as the port it runs on and the database-connection information. When you run the application locally during development, these variables are likely to be different from those on the production machine.

A common approach for dealing with this problem is to specify the environment variables outside the application and have it read them at runtime. In this section we'll see how we can read these variables from a Leiningen profile or the system environment.

Leiningen profiles allow managing many aspects of the application, such as dependencies, resource paths, and environment variables. You can create a separate profile for each scenario, and when the application is run using that profile it will have the correct environment information available to it.

The profiles can be specified either directly in the project.clj or in a separate profiles.clj file in the same location. The latter can be useful for any sensitive information you might not wish to check into version control. The profiles specified in profiles.clj will override those in project.clj.

Let's open the project.clj for the picture gallery. You'll notice that it already has *production* and *dev* profiles set up:

picture-gallery-logging/project.clj
```
:profiles
{:production
 {:ring
  {:open-browser? false, :stacktraces? false, :auto-reload? false}}
 :dev
 {:dependencies [[ring-mock "0.1.5"] [ring/ring-devel "1.2.0"]]}}
```

We'll update these profiles to add our environment variables:

```
:profiles
{:production
  {:ring {:open-browser? false,
          :stacktraces? false,
          :auto-reload? false}
   :env {:port 3000
         :db-url "//localhost/gallery"
         :db-user "admin"
         :db-pass "admin"
         :galleries-path "galleries"}}
  :dev
  {:dependencies [[ring-mock "0.1.5"]
                  [ring/ring-devel "1.2.0"]]
   :env {:port 3000
         :db-url "//localhost/gallery"
         :db-user "admin"
         :db-pass "secretProdPasword"
         :galleries-path "galleries"}}}
```

We'll use the Environ library to read the configuration variables from the profile. To use it we'll need to add the following dependency and plug-in to our project:

```
:dependencies [... [environ "0.4.0"]]
:plugins [... [lein-environ "0.4.0"]]
```

Now we can update our picture-gallery.models.db namespace to read the database configuration from the environment:

```
(ns picture-gallery.models.db
  (:require ...
            [environ.core :refer [env]]))

(def db
  {:subprotocol "postgresql"
   :subname (env :db-url)
   :user (env :db-user)
   :password (env :db-pass)}})
```

We can also update the picture-gallery.util/galleries variable to read the path from the envrionment.

```
(ns picture-gallery.util
  (:require [noir.session :as session]
            [hiccup.util :refer [url-encode]]
            [environ.core :refer [env]])
  (:import java.io.File))

...

(def galleries (env :galleries-path))
```

Unfortunately, if you're using Eclipse, the Counterclockwise plug-in will not load up the variables from the profile. Luckily, Environ can also read environment variables directly.

To add the variables, simply open Run Configuration in Eclipse and select our project. We can add these variables under the Environment tab. Next time we start the REPL, the environment variables will be available and Environ will pick them up.

Packaging Applications

Our application is now ready to be packaged and deployed. In this section we'll discuss how to accomplish this using Leiningen. As you'll see, this is a straightforward process. However, you need to be aware of a few things, depending on how you wish to run the application in production.

Up to this point we've been running our application in the REPL or by calling lein ring server to start up Jetty in development mode. In this mode the server watches the files for changes and reloads them as needed. This obviously causes a significant performance hit.

There are two ways to run Clojure web applications in production. Let's look at the benefits and drawbacks of these approaches.

The first approach is to create a standalone executable with an embedded server such as Jetty. This way the application will not have any external dependencies aside from having the Java runtime installed on the system.

The downside of this approach is that we'll have to manage all our configuration for the server manually. We'll have to configure our own logging, database connections, SSL configuration, and so on. It also means that each application will have more overhead, as we need to spawn an independent server for it.

The second approach is to create a web application archive (WAR) that can be deployed to an application server such as Tomcat. With this approach we can do all the environment-specific configuration on the application server. When the applications are deployed, they can read this configuration from the environment variables.

The application server can also host multiple applications on a shared domain. This allows us to have less overhead per application and the ability to provide a common confuguration for all the applications deployed on the server. The container can keep track of database connection settings, logging configurations, managing HTTPS listeners, and so on.

This approach is especially convenient if you're managing multiple applications and if you have separate environments for development, staging, and production. Since none of the configuration lives in the application, you don't need to have separate configurations when deploying to different environments.

The downside of this approach is that the application server will have higher overhead than embedded Jetty. The application server's configuration is often more complex, as well. The work involved may not be justified, depending on how you plan to manage your application in production.

The good news is that it's equally easy to package the application for either type of deployment. If you start with one approach you can switch to the other with minimal effort.

Standalone Deployment

Here, we'll take a closer look at what's involved in deployment as a standalone application.

Running as an Uberjar

When we wish to package the application for standalone deployment, we simply run the following from the application's root:

```
lein ring uberjar
```

The resulting artifact will be created in the target folder. We can now run this JAR by invoking java -jar picture-gallery-0.1.0-SNAPSHOT-standalone.jar. Once the server starts, you can see it running by browsing to localhost:3000.

The server runs on port 3000 by default. To override the default port use the $PORT environment variable.

Running with HTTP Kit

The uberjar we created uses an embedded Jetty server. However, it's possible to swap out Jetty for a different container. One such container is HTTP Kit.

HTTP Kit is a Ring-compliant event-driven server for Clojure that aims to be a drop-in replacement for Jetty. Unlike Jetty, HTTP Kit uses the non-blocking I/O model to handle requests. This allows for extremely high throughput and scalability.

To use HTTP Kit, we'll have to reference it in our project.clj dependencies and create our own main method.

```
:dependencies [... [http-kit "2.1.12"]]
```

Lein-ring currently doesn't support HTTP Kit, so we have to create our own main to run it. Let's create a new namespace called picture-gallery.main and add the following to it:

```
(ns picture-gallery.main
  (:use picture-gallery.handler
        [org.httpkit.server :only [run-server]]
        [ring.middleware file-info file])
  (:gen-class))
(defn -main [& [port]]
  (let [port (if port (Integer/parseInt port) 3000)]
    (run-server app {:port port})
    (println (str "You can view the site at http://localhost:" port))))
```

Our -main function will simply create an instance of the HTTP Kit server by running org.httpkit.server/run-server and passing it our app handler. The only thing to note here is that we *must* use the :gen-class hint in the namespace declaration to ensure that it gets compiled into Java bytecode.

Note that the hyphen (-) in front of -main indicates that this function will be accessible from Java. This is necessary since runnable Java programs require a main function entry point.

Next, we simply have to specify the main method in the project.clj by adding the following directive:

```
:main picture-gallery.main
```

We can now compile the application as a standalone executable and run it:

```
lein uberjar
java -jar target/picture-gallery-0.1.0-SNAPSHOT-standalone.jar
```

That's all there is to it. If your application requires the extra performance or any of the other HTTP Kit features, you can easily swap between it and Jetty.

Running with Leiningen Trampoline

Another way to run the application is by using lein trampoline that terminates the lein process after executing the command. We can do this as follows:

```
lein trampoline ring server-headless PORT
```

Here the PORT would have to be provided as an environment variable.

This method will use the configuration specified under the :ring key in the project.clj. For example, our picture gallery has the following configuration:

```
:ring {:handler picture-gallery.handler/app
       :init picture-gallery.handler/init
       :destroy picture-gallery.handler/destroy}
```

Using lein trampoline allows us to manage the application's complete life cycle via Leiningen.

Running as a Daemon

We can easily run our application as a daemon on *nix systems. For example, to daemonize it on Ubuntu, we could create an *upstart* configuration.[7] To do that we'll create a configuration file /etc/init/gallery.conf, where we'll add the following settings:

```
## Upstart config file (use 'start gallery', 'stop gallery')
## stdout and stderr will be captured in /var/log/upstart/gallery.log
author "Me"
description "Start the Picture Gallery webapp on its default port"
start on (local-filesystems and net-device-up IFACE!=lo)
exec java -jar /srv/gallery/picture-gallery-0.1.0-SNAPSHOT-standalone.jar

## Try to restart up to 10 times within 5 min:
respawn limit 10 300
```

Application-Server Deployment

Now that we know how to run our application standalone, let's see how that compares to running it on an application server.

---

7.   http://upstart.ubuntu.com/

Tomcat Deployment

To deploy your application on Tomcat you will need to download a copy of the Tomcat server and extract the archive locally.

You start Tomcat by running bin/catalina.sh start under the Tomcat directory. You can see the server logs under logs/catalina.out. When the server starts, you should see something like the following in your log:

```
May 5, 2013 11:12:25 AM org.apache.catalina.core.AprLifecycleListener init
INFO: The APR based Apache Tomcat Native library which allows optimal performance
in production environments was not found on the java.library.path:
.:/Library/Java/Extensions:/System/Library/Java/Extensions:/usr/lib/java
May 5, 2013 11:12:25 AM org.apache.coyote.AbstractProtocol init
INFO: Initializing ProtocolHandler ["http-bio-3000"]
...
```

Stopping the server is equally simple. To do that we run bin/catalina.sh stop.

To deploy our application as a WAR, we need to use the uberwar option:

```
lein ring uberwar
```

This will produce the deployable WAR artifact, which we can then deploy to the server. Deploying the application consists of copying the generated archive to the webapps directory under Tomcat.

When the application is deployed it will have a context relative to the server's root. By default the context is inferred from the archive name. Let's deploy the archive we created as picture-gallery.war

```
cp target/picture-gallery-0.1.0-SNAPSHOT-standalone.war \
~/tomcat/webapps/picture-gallery.war
```

The application should now be available at http://localhost:3000/picture-gallery.

Note that it's also possible to deploy the application at the server's root. To do that we have to name the archive ROOT.war.

Immutant Deployment

Another great option for deployment is Immutant. It's an application server designed specifically for hosting Clojure applications, and it provides its own Leiningen integration. We can even install Immutant via Leiningen by running the following command:

```
lein immutant install 1.0.2
```

Once Immutant is installed, we can simply run the following from our application's root directory:

```
lein immutant deploy
```

Launching the Immutant server is equally easy using the following:

```
lein immutant run
```

The approaches we've discussed require us to manage our own server. An alternative is to deploy the application on a cloud service. Heroku in particular provides explicit support for running Clojure applications. In the following section we'll look at how to deploy our application there.

Heroku Deployment

Heroku is a cloud service with a free hosting option. Before we start using Heroku we need to make sure we have Git and Heroku Toolbelt installed.[8,9]

Heroku uses the command specified in a file called Procfile to start up the application. This file must be placed in the project's root directory.

A common way to run a Clojure application on Heroku is by using the Leiningen trampoline option we discussed earlier. To do that we add the following directive in the Procfile:

```
web: lein with-profile production trampoline ring server
```

Next we need to initialize a Git repository for our application by running the following commands:

```
git init
git add .
git commit -m "init"
```

Once our repository is created, we can test the application by running foreman start. If the application starts up fine, then we're ready to deploy it to the cloud by running the following command:

```
heroku create
```

To add Postgres support for the application, we run this command:

```
heroku addons:add heroku-postgresql
```

You can find the connection settings for the database on your Heroku dashboard. You'll need to add these to your database configuration in the application. We're now ready to push our application to Heroku:

```
git push heroku master
```

---

8. http://git-scm.com/
9. https://toolbelt.heroku.com/

Once the upload completes, Heroku will attempt to build and deploy your application. If this process completes successfully, you should be able to browse to the application URL specified in your administration console.

What You've Learned

This concludes the design, implementation, and deployment of our site. While building and designing it we covered many aspects of creating a real-world application, such as handling static resources, database access, and Ajax.

I hope these steps were easy to follow and you'll be able to apply them in building real-world applications with Clojure.

Although our site is functional, it clearly could use some improvements. You may wish to consider implementing paging for large galleries, creation of multiple galleries per user, upload of multiple images in batches, and setting the visibility of uploaded images.

So far we've covered only a single set of libraries for developing web applications. However, the Clojure web stack is very flexible, and it's easy to swap individual pieces for others. In the next chapter we'll cover how to update the picture gallery to use the Selmer templating engine, ClojureScript, and SQL Korma.

CHAPTER 7

Mixing It Up

In this chapter we'll see several alternative ways to write the picture-gallery application from Chapter 5, *Picture Gallery*, on page 81. We'll cover how to swap the HTML templating engines, use ClojureScript, and write SQL queries using the Korma domain-specific language (DSL).

Using Selmer

In Chapter 2, *Clojure Web Stack*, on page 25, I mentioned that there's a number of templating languages available for Clojure. In this section we'll look at the Selmer engine and see what's involved in converting our picture gallery to use it instead of Hiccup.[1]

The reason for picking Selmer over some of the more popular alternatives, such as Enlive, is its ease of use and familiarity. Enlive has a steep learning curve and can be difficult to master.

On the other hand, Selmer is based on the Django templating engine.[2] If you're already familiar with Django or similar templating languages, you should feel right at home. Another advantage to using Selmer is that it's fast.

What's Different about Selmer?

Hiccup is a nice and simple templating engine. Unfortunately, its biggest advantage is also its greatest weakness. Since Hiccup templates are written using Clojure data structures, they're simply part of your regular code.

This makes the templates inaccessible to people not versed in Clojure. For example, you can't just give a designer your template to work with.

---

1. https://github.com/yogthos/Selmer
2. https://docs.djangoproject.com/en/dev/ref/templates/

Another issue is that it makes it easy for your front-end and back-end logic to bleed into each other if you're not careful. Finally, you have to redeploy your site any time you wish to make a change to the layout.

Selmer provides a powerful mini language that can be used for general-purpose templating. When applied to generating HTML templates it encourages a clean separation between the presentation and the business logic. On top of that, the templates can be maintained by somebody without any knowledge of Clojure.

Creating Templates

The templates are simply HTML files with additional template tags. Let's look at an example template:

```
<html>
  <head>
    <meta http-equiv="Content-Type" content="text/html; charset=UTF-8"/>
    <title>My First Template</title>
  </head>
  <body>
    <h2>Hello {{name}}</h2>
  </body>
</html>
```

The templates are rendered using a context represented by a map. The context contains any variables that we'd like to render in our template. In the previous code, we have a template representing a page that renders a single variable called name.

There are two functions for rendering templates, called render and render-file. The render function accepts a string representing the template. The render-file function accepts a string representing the path to the file containing the template.

If we saved the template defined earlier in a file called index.html, then we could render it as follows:

```
(ns example.routes.home
  (:require [selmer.parser :refer [render-file]]))

(defn index [request]
  (render-file "example/views/templates/index.html"
               {:name "John"}))
```

The render-file function expects the first argument to be a path to the template. The path should be relative to the application's src folder. The second parameter is the map representing the context for the template.

In the preceding code we passed in a string as the value for the variable name. However, we're not restricted to strings and can pass in any type we like. For example, if we pass in a collection we can iterate it using the for tag:

```
<ul>
{% for item in items %}
<li> {{item}} </li>
{% endfor %}
</ul>

(render-file "/example/views/templates/items.html
              {:items (range 10)})
```

If an item happens to be a map, we can access the keys by name, as follows:

```
(render "<p>Hello {{user.first}} {{user.last}}</p>"
        {:user {:first "John" :last "Doe"}})
```

When no special processing is specified in the template, the parameter's .toString value will be used.

Using Filters

Filters allow for postprocessing the variables before they are rendered. For example, you can use a filter to convert the variable to uppercase, compute a hash, or count the length. Filters are specified by using a pipe symbol (|) after the variable name, as seen here:

```
{{name|upper}}
```

Selmer comes with a number of handy filters, such as upper, date, and pluralize, out of the box. On top of that we can easily define our own filters using the selmer.filters/add-filter! function:

```
(add-filter! :empty? empty?)

(render "{% if files|empty? %}no files{% else %}files{% endif %}"
  {:files []})
```

By default the content of the filters will be escaped; we can override this behavior as follows:

```
(add-filter! :foo
  (fn [x] [:safe (.toUpperCase x)]))

(render "{{x|foo}}" {:x "<div>I'm safe</div>"})
```

Using Template Tags

Selmer provides two types of tags. The first kind are inline tags such as extends and include. These tags are self-contained statements and do not require an end tag. The other type are the block tags. These tags have a start and an end tag, and operate on a block of text. An example of this would be the if ... endif block.

Defining Custom Tags

In addition to tags already provided, you can easily define custom tags by using the selmer.parser/add-tag! macro. Let's look at an example to see how it works:

```
(add-tag!
 :image
 (fn [args context-map]
    (str "<img src=" (first args) "/>")))
```

```
(render "{% image \"http://foo.com/logo.jpg\" %}" {})
```

We can also define a block tag by using the overloaded add-tag! definition. In this case we will provide the opening tag, followed by the handler function and any closing tags. The handler will accept an addition parameter that holds the content of each block. The content will be keyed on the name of the block, as in the following example:

```
(add-tag! :uppercase
          (fn [args context-map content]
             (.toUpperCase (get-in content [:uppercase :content])))
          :enduppercase)
```

```
(render "{% uppercase %}foo {{bar}} baz{% enduppercase %}" {:bar "injected"})
```

Inheriting Templates

Selmer templates can refer to other templates using the block tag. There are two ways to refer to a template. We can either extend templates using the extends tag or include templates with the include tag.

Extending Templates

When we use the extends tag, the current template will use the template it's extending as the base. Any blocks in the base template with the names matching the current template will be overwritten.

Let's look at a concrete example. First, we'll define our base template and call it base.html:

```
<!DOCTYPE html>
<head>
    <link rel="stylesheet" href="style.css" />
    <title>{% block title %}My amazing site{% endblock %}</title>
</head>
```

```
<body>
    <div id="content">
        {% block content %}{% endblock %}
    </div>
</body>
</html>
```

Then we'll create a new template called home.html that will extend base.html as follows:

```
{% extends "base.html" %}

{% block content %}
    {% for entry in entries %}
        <h2>{{ entry.title }}</h2>
        <p>{{ entry.body }}</p>
    {% endfor %}
{% endblock %}
```

When the home.html is rendered the content block will display the entries defined there. However, since we did not define a block for the title, the one from base.html will be used.

Note that you can chain extended templates together. In this case the latest occurrence of a block tag will be the one that's rendered.

Including Templates

The include tag allows including content from other templates in the current template. Let's look at an example. Say we have a base.html template that includes templates named register.html and home.html, then defines blocks called register and home:

```
<!DOCTYPE html>
<head>
    <link rel="stylesheet" href="style.css" />
    <title>{% block title %}My amazing site{% endblock %}</title>
</head>

<body>
    <div id="content">
        {% if user %}
            {% include "home.html" %}
        {% else %}
            {% include "register.html" %}
        {% endif %}
    </div>
</body>
</html>
```

We can now define the content for these tags in separate template files called home.html and register.html, respectively:

```
<h1>Hello {{user}}</h1>

<form action="/register" method="POST">
    <label for="id">user id</label>
    <input id="id" name="id" type="text"></input>
    <input pass="pass" name="pass" type="text"></input>
    <input type="submit" value="register">
</form>
```

When the base.html is rendered it will replace the include tags with the content from the included templates.

Converting the Picture Gallery to Selmer

As we've seen, Selmer uses plain HTML to define the pages. Our first step will be to identify the parts of the application responsible for rendering the pages and convert them accordingly.

Let's see what routes our application has, and which of these are responsible for serving up the pages:

The home namespace contains a single route to render the home page:

- GET "/"

The gallery namespace contains a route for displaying the gallery for a specific user:

- GET "/gallery/:userid"

The upload namespace contains routes to upload and delete images. Only one of these routes is responsible for serving a page:

- GET "/upload"
- POST "/upload"
- POST "/delete"

Finally, the auth namespace contains routes for registration, authentication, and account management:

- GET "/register"
- POST "/register"
- POST "/login"
- GET "/logout"
- GET "/delete-account"
- POST "/confirm-delete"

As you can see, only a few routes are responsible for displaying pages. This makes our task relatively simple.

We'll open up our project.clj and add the Selmer [selmer "0.5.4"] dependency to it.

Next, we'll create a picture-gallery.views.templates namespace. This is where all the Selmer templates will live.

Our current layout uses Hiccup to create the page skeleton and render the content of our pages using it. Now we can update our layout namespace to render the templates instead.

As you'll recall, Selmer uses an HTML template and a map of parameters to process it. We'll replace the common helper in our layout with a render function that will take care of rendering the templates. To do that we'll reference the selmer.parser namespace in the layout declaration:

```clojure
(ns picture-gallery.views.layout
    (:require [selmer.parser :as parser]))
```

Then we'll define the path to our templates and write a helper function to render our templates. This function will take care of prepending the template path, adding the Servlet context key, and setting the user from the session.

Putting all the boilerplate in the layout will allow us to focus on the parameters relevant to the task we're working on when rendering the templates.

picture-gallery-selmer/src/picture_gallery/views/layout.clj
```clojure
(def template-folder "picture_gallery/views/templates/")

(defn utf-8-response [html]
  (content-type (response html) "text/html; charset=utf-8"))

(deftype RenderablePage [template params]
  Renderable
  (render [this request]
    (->> (assoc params
                :context (:context request)
                :user    (session/get :user))

         (parser/render-file (str template-folder template))
         utf-8-response)))

(defn render [template & [params]]
  (RenderablePage. template params))
```

Now that we've updated the layout, let's create a base template for our pages. We'll call this file base.html and put it in the src/picture_gallery/views/templates/ folder.

picture-gallery-selmer/src/picture_gallery/views/templates/base.html

```html
<html>
<head>
<title>Welcome to picture-gallery</title>
<link href="{{context}}/css/screen.css" rel="stylesheet" type="text/css" />
<script type="text/javascript">
    var context = "{{context}}";
</script>
<script src="//code.jquery.com/jquery-2.0.2.min.js" type="text/javascript"></script>
<script src="{{context}}/js/colors.js" type="text/javascript"></script>
<script src="{{context}}/js/site.js" type="text/javascript"></script>
</head>
<body>
  {% block menu %}
  <div id="usermenu">
    <div class="menuitem"><a href="/">home</a></div>
    {% if user %}
    <div class="menuitem">
     <a href="/upload">upload images</a>
    </div>
    <div class="menuitem">
      <a href="/logout">logout {{user}}</a>
    </div>
    <div class="menuitem">
      <a href="/delete-account">delete account</a>
    </div>
    {% else %}
    <div class="menuitem">
      <a href="{{context}}/register">register</a>
    </div>
    <div class="menuitem">
      <form action="{{context}}/login" method="POST">
        <input id="id"
               name="id"
               placeholder="screen name"
               type="text">
        <input id="pass"
               name="pass"
               placeholder="password"
               type="password">
        <input type="submit" value="login">
      </form>
    </div>
    {% endif %}
  </div>
    {% endblock %}
    {% block content %}
    {% endblock %}
</body>
</html>
```

The base template fills the same role as the common function in the Hiccup version of the application. It creates the base layout and includes the necessary resources. The pages can then extend the template and add their contents inside the content block. Note that we have to use the Servlet context to ensure that the local resources are accessible when the application is deployed on an application server.

Converting the Home Page

Let's create a new template called home.html and update our home page to use this template to render its contents. The home template will extend the base we created earlier and then create the thumbnail links for each gallery. This template replaces the functionality of the show-galleries function in the gallery namespace.

picture-gallery-selmer/src/picture_gallery/views/templates/home.html
```
{% extends "picture_gallery/views/templates/base.html" %}
{% block content %}
<div class="gallery">
  {% for gallery in galleries %}
  <div class="thumbnail">
    <a href="{{context}}/gallery/{{gallery.userid}}">
      <img
        src="{{context}}/img/{{gallery.userid}}/{{thumb-prefix}}{{gallery.name}}"/>
        {{gallery.userid}}'s gallery
    </a>
  </div>
  {% endfor %}
</div>
{% endblock %}
```

With our templates in place, we can now update our home route to use the render function we defined in layout. Previously, we used show-galleries from the gallery namespace to render the picture galleries. We can now grab the list of galleries directly from the db namespace and let the template render them.

picture-gallery-selmer/src/picture_gallery/routes/home.clj
```
(ns picture-gallery.routes.home
  (:require [compojure.core :refer [defroutes GET]]
            [picture-gallery.views.layout :as layout]
            [picture-gallery.util :refer [thumb-prefix]]
            [picture-gallery.models.db :as db]
            [noir.session :as session]))
(defn home []
  (layout/render "home.html"
                 {:thumb-prefix thumb-prefix
                  :galleries    (db/get-gallery-previews)}))
(defroutes home-routes
  (GET "/" [] (home)))
```

If we reload our home page we should see the thumbnails for the galleries just as we did before.

The next step is to create a template to display the thumbnails for each individual gallery. To do this, we'll create a new file called gallery.html in our templates package. This template will display a thumbnail with a link for each image in the user's gallery.

picture-gallery-selmer/src/picture_gallery/views/templates/gallery.html

```
{% extends "picture_gallery/views/templates/base.html" %}

{% block content %}
<div class="gallery">
   <div id="error"></div>
   <script src="{{context}}/js/gallery.js" type="text/javascript"></script>
   <div>
   {% for pic in pictures %}
      <div class="thumbnail">
         <a class={{pic.name}} href="{{context}}/img/{{pic.userid}}/{{pic.name}}">
            <img src="{{context}}/img/{{pic.userid}}/{{thumb-prefix}}{{pic.name}}"/>
            {% ifequal user page-owner %}
            <input id="{{pic.name}}"
                   name="{{pic.name}}"
                   type="checkbox"
                   value="true" />
            {% endifequal %}
            </a>
      </div>
   {% endfor %}
   {% ifequal user page-owner %}
      <input id="delete" type="submit" value="delete images" />
   {% endifequal %}
   </div>
</div>
{% endblock %}
```

As you can see, the template is very similar to the one for home, except that it now includes the script for gallery management and the thumbnails link to the full images.

We can now update our gallery namespace to use the Selmer template for rendering the user galleries.

picture-gallery-selmer/src/picture_gallery/routes/gallery.clj

```
(ns picture-gallery.routes.gallery
  (:require [compojure.core :refer [defroutes GET]]
            [picture-gallery.views.layout :as layout]
            [picture-gallery.util :refer [thumb-prefix]]
            [picture-gallery.models.db :as db]
            [noir.session :as session]))
```

```
(defn display-gallery [userid]
  (layout/render "gallery.html"
                 {:thumb-prefix thumb-prefix
                  :page-owner   userid
                  :pictures     (db/images-by-user userid)}))

(defroutes gallery-routes
  (GET "/gallery/:userid" [userid]
       (display-gallery userid)))
```

You'll notice that as we move our rendering logic to the templates the application code shrinks dramatically.

The remaining tasks are to create templates for user registration and file uploads. Let's see how we can accomplish these.

Converting the Registration Pages

In the auth namespace, we have two functions responsible for rendering pages for registration and account deletion. We'll create separate templates for each of these pages.

The registration page is rather straightforward. It's simply a form for the user to input her ID and set a password. We'll extend our base layout and add this form to our content block. Let's call this template registration.html. Notice that we provide an empty block for the menu so that it's not rendered on this page.

picture-gallery-selmer/src/picture_gallery/views/templates/registration.html

```
{% extends "picture_gallery/views/templates/base.html" %}
{% block menu %}
{% endblock %}
{% block content %}
<div class="content">
    <form action="{{context}}/register" method="POST">

        <label for="user-id">user id</label>
        <input id="id"
               name="id"
               tabindex="1"
               type="text"
               value="{{id}}" /><br />
        <div class="error">{{id-error}}</div>

        <label for="pass">password</label>
        <input id="pass"
               name="pass"
               tabindex="2"
               type="password" /><br />
        <div class="error">{{pass-error}}</div>
```

```
            <label for="pass1">retype password</label>
            <input id="pass1"
                   name="pass1"
                   tabindex="3"
                   type="password" /><br />
            <input tabindex="4" type="submit" value="create account" />
        </form>
    </div>
{% endblock %}
```

The account-deletion page looks very similar, except here we have the forms
to confirm deletion or abort. We'll name this template deleteAccount.html.

picture-gallery-selmer/src/picture_gallery/views/templates/deleteAccount.html
```
{% extends "picture_gallery/views/templates/base.html" %}
{% block content %}
<div class="gallery">
    <form action="{{context}}/confirm-delete" method="POST">
        <input type="submit" value="delete account" />
    </form>
    <form action="{{context}}/" method="GET">
        <input type="submit" value="cancel" />
    </form>
</div>
{% endblock %}
```

Meanwhile, our route handlers for the /register and /delete-account URLs simply
render their respective templates:

picture-gallery-selmer/src/picture_gallery/routes/auth.clj
```
(defn registration-page [& [id]]
  (layout/render "registration.html"
                 {:id id
                  :id-error (first (vali/get-errors :id))
                  :pass-error (first (vali/get-errors :pass))}))
```

Converting the Upload Page

Once again, we'll start by designing our page template and then make changes
to the code to accommodate it.

picture-gallery-selmer/src/picture_gallery/views/templates/upload.html
```
{% extends "picture_gallery/views/templates/base.html" %}

{% block content %}
<div class="gallery">
        <h2>Upload an image</h2>
        {% if error %}
        <p class="error">{{error}}</p>
        {% endif %}
```

```
        {% if image %}
        <img src={{image}} width="300" height="300"/>
        {% endif %}

        <form action="{{context}}/upload"
              enctype="multipart/form-data"
              method="POST">
            <input id="file"
                   name="file"
                   type="file" />
            <input type="submit" value="upload" />
        </form>
</div>
{% endblock %}
```

Here we create the form to upload the image, and placeholders to display the result of the upload action. If the upload is successful then a link to the thumbnail is returned; otherwise the service will return some error text.

We'll now have to make a few tweaks to the upload namespace to use the template:

picture-gallery-selmer/src/picture_gallery/routes/upload.clj
```
(defn upload-page [params]
  (layout/render "upload.html" params))


(defn handle-upload [{:keys [filename] :as file}]
  (upload-page
    (if (empty? filename)
      {:error "please select a file to upload"}
      (try
        (upload-file (gallery-path) file)
        (save-thumbnail file)
        (db/add-image (session/get :user) filename)
        {:image (thumb-uri (session/get :user) filename)}
        (catch Exception ex
          (error ex "an error has occured while uploading" name)
          {:error (str "error uploading file " (.getMessage ex))})))))
```

picture-gallery-selmer/src/picture_gallery/routes/upload.clj
```
(defroutes upload-routes
  (GET "/img/:user-id/:file-name" [user-id file-name]
       (serve-file user-id file-name))

  (GET "/upload" [info] (restricted (upload-page {:info info})))

  (POST "/upload" [file] (restricted (handle-upload file)))

  (POST "/delete" [names] (restricted (delete-images names))))
```

As you can see, we were able to switch our templating engines with minimal effort. Both Hiccup and Selmer offer their own benefits.

Upgrading to ClojureScript

Up to now, we've been using Clojure exclusively on the server, and plain old JavaScript for our client-side logic. ClojureScript is a dialect of Clojure that compiles to JavaScript. This allows us to use the same language for both the client and the server. Not only that, but it's even possible to share code between the two.

Let's look at why we might wish to use ClojureScript for front-end development. If you've worked with JavaScript you've probably noticed that it has many shortcomings. Let's look at some of these and how ClojureScript addresses them.

JavaScript syntax is full of quirks and it's easy to write code that looks like it's doing one thing, but in fact does something else entirely. Equality checks are a good example. Since there are different rules for equality depending on the type of data, it's easy to make a mistake. It also leads to ugly code such as the following example:

```
if (typeof my_var !== "undefined" && my_var !== null) {
  // wow, that's ugly!
}
```

JavaScript code can be fairly verbose and it doesn't lend itself well to metaprogramming. It takes a needless amount of effort to organize your code, as there is no built-in support for namespacing.

The conventions for what constitutes proper code differ wildly between libraries and development shops. Some people write functional-style JavaScript, and others use it to write object-oriented code. A lot of the time these conventions don't mesh well together.

There is no Leiningen equivalent for JavaScript. This means that you have to manually keep track of dependencies and libraries.

For these reasons, it takes a lot of effort and discipline to write robust Java-Script programs. However, JavaScript does have the advantage of being a standard programmable environment for all modern browsers. Since it's become the de facto standard for the client side, JavaScript engines have been improving their performance dramatically in recent years.

It would be nice to leverage this platform with a robust programming language like Clojure. This is precisely where ClojureScript comes into play.

In addition to addressing these problems, ClojureScript brings the advantage of using the same language for both the client and the server. This means we can share logic between the two without having to write it twice and potentially introduce errors and inconsistencies.

Much like its cousin Clojure, ClojureScript embraces its hosting platform and allows seamless interop with JavaScript. We can continue leveraging mature JavaScript libraries while enjoying the benefits of Clojure language semantics.

ClojureScript Overview

You should be aware of a couple of points when using ClojureScript. Since ClojureScript runs in the browser, we cannot leverage any code that relies on interfacing with Java. Only libraries written in pure Clojure can be shared. The syntax for interop with JavaScript is also slightly different from that for interacting with Java.

JavaScript Interop

Interacting with JavaScript turns out to be remarkably simple. Any standard JavaScript functions can be accessed using the js namespace. For example, if we want to make a logger that logs to the console, we can write something like the following:

```
(defn log [& items]
  (.log js/console (apply str items)))
```

One thing that's not obvious is the interaction with JavaScript object properties. To access these we use (.-property obj) notation, where the hyphen (-) indicates that we're referencing a property and not a function. We update properties by calling the set! function. Here's an example:

```
(defn init []
  (let [canvas (.getElementById js/document "canvas")
        ctx    (.getContext canvas "2d")
        width  (.-width canvas)
        height (.-height canvas)]
    (log "width: " width " height: " height)
    ;;set a property
    (set! (.-fillStyle ctx) "black")
    (.fillRect ctx 0 0 width height)))
```

Macros

Another area where ClojureScript differs from Clojure is that you have to reference macros with :require-macros keyword in your namespace declaration:

```
(ns my.app
  (:require-macros [app.macros :as m]))
```

Note that the :as declaration is required when referencing macros.

Concurrency

While ClojureScript supports atoms, there is no Software Transactional Memory and therefore there are no refs or agents. The binding semantics are slightly different, as well, because there are no Vars or runtime reification.

Finally, there is no runtime evaluation or compilation in ClojureScript. Aside from these differences, development in ClojureScript is very similar to that in regular Clojure.

Let's look at what's involved in porting the JavaScript code for our gallery to ClojureScript. The easiest way to add ClojureScript support to the project is to use the lein-cljsbuild plug-in.[3] With it you can specify the ClojureScript sources, the Clojure namespaces you'd like to reference, and the JavaScript files to output.

We'll first need to add the ClojureScript library and the Leiningen plug-in to our project by adding the following to our project.clj:

```
:dependencies [...
               [org.clojure/tools.reader "0.7.10"]
               [org.clojure/clojurescript "0.0-1806"]]
:plugins [... [lein-cljsbuild "0.3.2"]]
:cljsbuild
{:builds
  [{:source-paths ["src-cljs"]
    :compiler
    {:pretty-print false
     :output-to "resources/public/js/gallery-cljs.js"}}]}
```

The configuration under :cljsbuild specifies that the ClojureScript code will live in the src-cljs source folder. The compiled ClojureScript will be output to the gallery-cljs.js file in our project's resources/public/js/ directory.

Let's create the src-cljs directory in our project's root. We'll follow the same naming convention as we did with JavaScript and create gallery.cljs and site.cljs namespaces there.

Note that ClojureScript files must end with the .cljs extension. If you use the .clj extension the compiler will still attempt to compile the namespace, but will not be able to interoperate with JavaScript. This means you'll get errors trying to call any native JavaScript functions.

There are two options for invoking ClojureScript compilation using lein. We can either run lein cljsbuild once or lein cljsbuild auto. When using the auto option, the build will watch for changes in the source and automatically recompile

---

3.   https://github.com/emezeske/lein-cljsbuild

them as needed. This takes much less time than compiling using the once
option, and turns out to be quite handy for development.

If we wish to remove any artifacts created by previous builds we can run lein
cljsbuild clean to do that.

We'll use the Domina library for manipulating the document-object model
(DOM) elements and handling events, and cljs-ajax to handle our Ajax calls.[4,5]
We can include these libraries just like any other dependency in our project.clj.

```
:dependencies [...
               [domina "1.0.0"]
               [cljs-ajax "0.2.0"]]
```

At this point we're ready to start the ClojureScript compiler by running the
following:

```
lein cljsbuild auto
```

Once the auto build is running, any changes we make to the namespaces in
the src-clj source folder will be recompiled and become available in the browser
when the page is reloaded.

First, let's see what our current JavaScript code looks like in site.sj.

picture-gallery-selmer/resources/public/js/site.js
```javascript
function colorStr(color) {
    return "rgb("+color[0]+","+color[1]+","+color[2]+")";
}
function setColor(div, colors) {
    var bgColor = colors[0];
    var textColor = colors[1];
    div.css("background-color", colorStr(bgColor));
    div.find('a').css("color", colorStr(textColor));
}
$(document).ready(function(){
    $(".thumbnail")
            .each(function() {
            var div = $(this);
            var url = div.find('img').attr('src');
            var thumbColors = new AlbumColors(url);
            var color = "";
            thumbColors.getColors(function(colors) {
            setColor(div, colors);
        });
    });
});
```

---

4.   https://github.com/levand/domina
5.   https://github.com/yogthos/cljs-ajax

Here, we use the AlbumColors library to find colors to use as the background and foreground of the div containing our thumbnail. Let's see how to call this library from ClojureScript instead.

picture-gallery-cljs/src-cljs/site.cljs

```clojure
(ns site
  (:require [domina :refer [by-class nodes sel attr]]
            [domina.css :refer [sel]]))

(defn rgb-str [[r g b]]
  (str "rgb(" r "," g "," b ")"))

(defn set-color [style foreground background]
  (set! (.-color style) (rgb-str foreground))
  (set! (.-backgroundColor style) (rgb-str background)))

(defn img-url [div]
  (-> div (sel "img") (attr "src")))

(defn set-colors [div]
  (.getColors (js/AlbumColors. (img-url div))
    (fn [[background _ foreground]]
      (set-color (.-style div) foreground background))))

(defn ^:export init []
  (doseq [div (nodes (by-class "thumbnail"))]
    (set-colors div)))
```

As you can see, the code is quite similar to the JavaScript version. One major difference is that we have to use an init function to hook into ClojureScript. Notice that it has the ^:export annotation. We need this annotation to protect the function name during advanced compilation. By default the Closure compiler will munge the names to shorten the resulting code.

We'll now update our base.html template to call the compiled gallery-cljs.js script. We'll also remove references to the old site.js, gallery.js scripts, and jQuery, as they're no longer necessary.

```html
<!DOCTYPE HTML>
<html>
    ...
        <script src="{{context}}/js/gallery-cljs.js" type="text/javascript">
        </script>
        <script>
            site.init();
        </script>
    </body>
</html>
```

Note that all our ClojureScript namespaces will be compiled to a single JavaScript output file. The content for both the site and the gallery will live in the same file, which gets loaded once.

Now let's look at converting the gallery.js to ClojureScript. Here we'll make Ajax calls using the cljs-ajax library.

The gallery.js script looks as follows:

```
picture-gallery-selmer/resources/public/js/gallery.js
$(document).ready(function(){
    $("#delete").click(deleteImages);
});
function deleteImages() {
    var selectedInputs = $("input:checked");
    var selectedIds = [];
    selectedInputs
    .each(function() {
            selectedIds.push($(this).attr('id'));
        });
    if (selectedIds.length < 1) alert("no images selected");
    else
        $.post(context + "/delete",
            {names: selectedIds},
            function(response) {
                var errors = $('<ul>');
                $.each(response, function() {
                if("ok" === this.status) {
                    var element = document.getElementById(this.name);
                    $(element).parent().parent().remove();
                }
                else
                    errors
                    .append($('<li>',
                            {html: "failed to remove " +
                                    this.name +
                                    ": " +
                                    this.status}));
                });
                if (errors.length > 0)
                    $('#error').empty().append(errors);
            },
            "json");
}
```

The script handles deleting the images from the user gallery and updating the page based on the server response. Let's open gallery.cljs and update the namespace definition to reference the required libraries:

```
picture-gallery-cljs/src-cljs/gallery.cljs
(ns gallery
  (:require [goog.dom :as dom]
            [domina :refer [by-id nodes append!]]
            [domina.events :refer [listen!]]
            [domina.css :refer [sel]]
            [ajax.core :refer [POST]]))
```

Since we only want to load our gallery-related functions on the gallery page, we'll create an init function for it. The function will bind the click event for the Delete button.

```
(defn ^:export init []
  (listen! (by-id "delete") :click deleteImages))
```

We now need to call gallery.init() in our page, but *after* the gallery-cljs.js script is loaded. To facilitate that we'll create a new scripts block in our base.html to allow pages to add their scripts there.

```
<html>
  <head>
  ...
  </head>
  <body>
  ...
  {% block scripts %}
  {% endblock %}
  </body>
</html>
```

Then in our gallery.html we'll call the init script:

```
{% extends "picture_gallery/views/templates/base.html" %}
...
{% block scripts %}
<script>
  gallery.init();
</script>
{% endblock %}
```

Let's look at how to implement the deleteImages function. First, we have to select all the checked inputs by using a CSS selector. We then grab the nodes from the resulting query. We'd like to grab each node's name property and return it. If we didn't find any checked inputs, we'll return a nil instead.

```
(defn find-selected []
  (->> (sel "input:checked")
       nodes
       (map #(.-name %))
       not-empty))
```

In deleteImages we'll try to find the selected check boxes using the find-selected we just wrote, and show an error if none are found. If any images are selected, we'd like to POST their names to the server.

picture-gallery-cljs/src-cljs/gallery.cljs
```
(defn deleteImages [_]
  (if-let [selected (find-selected)]
    (POST "/delete" {:params {:names selected}
                      :handler handle-response})
    (js/alert "no images selected")))
```

The response handler will check the status for each item and either remove it from the DOM or display the associated error, as was the case with our JavaScript version.

picture-gallery-cljs/src-cljs/gallery.cljs
```
(defn handle-response [response]
  (let [errors (goog.string.StringBuffer. "")]
    (doseq [{:keys [name status]} response]
      (if (= "ok" status)
        (-> (by-id name)
            (.-parentNode)
            (.-parentNode)
            (dom/removeNode))
        (.append errors (str "<li>failed to remove " name ": " status "</li>"))))
    (let [error-str (str "<ul>" (.toString errors) "</ul>")]
      (if (not-empty error-str)
        (append! (by-id "error") error-str)))))
```

The final rewrite of the JavaScript version should look like this:

picture-gallery-cljs/src-cljs/gallery.cljs
```
(ns gallery
  (:require [goog.dom :as dom]
            [domina :refer [by-id nodes append!]]
            [domina.events :refer [listen!]]
            [domina.css :refer [sel]]
            [ajax.core :refer [POST]]))

(defn handle-response [response]
  (let [errors (goog.string.StringBuffer. "")]
    (doseq [{:keys [name status]} response]
      (if (= "ok" status)
        (-> (by-id name)
            (.-parentNode)
            (.-parentNode)
            (dom/removeNode))
        (.append errors (str "<li>failed to remove " name ": " status "</li>"))))
    (let [error-str (str "<ul>" (.toString errors) "</ul>")]
      (if (not-empty error-str)
        (append! (by-id "error") error-str)))))
```

```
(defn find-selected []
  (->> (sel "input:checked")
       nodes
       (map #(.-name %))
       not-empty))

(defn deleteImages [_]
  (if-let [selected (find-selected)]
    (POST "/delete" {:params {:names selected}
                     :handler handle-response})
    (js/alert "no images selected")))
(defn ^:export init []
  (listen! (by-id "delete") :click deleteImages))
```

As you can see, using ClojureScript for client-side logic is very straightforward.

Since we're using ClojureScript we can use the Extensible Data Notation (EDN) format to transfer data between the client and the server.[6] This allows us to use regular Clojure data structures without having to encode them using an intermediate JavaScript Object Notation. To use it we'll need to include the *ring-middleware-format* middleware to handle the EDN-encoded requests.[7]

```
:dependencies [...
               [ring-middleware-format "0.3.1"]]
```

The POST function in the cljs-ajax library happens to use EDN as its default format. The only change we need to make is to add the middleware to our handler. We first reference it in the namespace declaration:

```
(ns picture-gallery.handler
  (:require
    ...
    [ring.middleware.format :refer [wrap-restful-format]]))
```

Then we simply pass the middleware to our app definition:

picture-gallery-cljs/src/picture_gallery/handler.clj
```
(def app (noir-middleware/app-handler
           [auth-routes
            home-routes
            upload-routes
            gallery-routes
            app-routes]
           :middleware [wrap-restful-format]
           :access-rules [user-page]))
```

---

6. https://github.com/edn-format/edn
7. https://github.com/ngrunwald/ring-middleware-format

The middleware will read the body of any EDN-encoded requests and set it as the :params key on the request.

So far we've been compiling our ClojureScript without any optimizations. If we look at the resulting script we see that it weighs in at around 1MB! Cleary, that wouldn't be acceptable for production use. To bring the size down to a more reasonable number we need to enable the advanced optimizations.

At this point we'll create separate profiles for dev and production builds. To do that we need to update our project.clj as follows:

```
:cljsbuild
  {:builds
    {:dev {:source-paths ["src-cljs"]
           :compiler
           {:pretty-print true
            :output-to "resources/public/js/gallery-cljs.js"}}
     :prod {:source-paths ["src-cljs"]
            :compiler
            {:optimizations :advanced
             :output-to "resources/public/js/gallery-cljs.js"}}}}
```

The development profile outputs more readable JavaScript that is easier to debug and does not attempt to optimize it. The production profile will munge variable names and apply advanced optimizations to keep the script size down as much as possible.

We can now build each profile explicitly by specifying it as an argument to cljsbuild:

```
lein cljsbuild once prod
```

However, when we compile the production ClojureScript and navigate to our page, we'll see an error that looks like this:

```
Uncaught TypeError: Object [object Object] has no method 'Le'
```

Unfortunately, the error is not terribly descriptive and doesn't give us much to go on. It says that we tried to call a method named Le on some object and that it doesn't exist.

The hint here is that we never defined a method called Le. The advanced optimizer will munge the function names. This isn't a problem for functions we've defined ourselves, as they're guaranteed to get consistent naming throughout. However, we're also calling a function from the AlbumColors library. The compiler will also munge its name, and the resulting name will obviously not be found.

Luckily, there's a simple solution to this problem. The Google Closure compiler provides a way to protect function names in external libraries by declaring them in an externs file. We'll create a new file called externs.js under the resources directory of our project. Then we'll declare the functions whose names we wish to protect in it:

```
picture-gallery-korma/resources/externs.js
var AlbumColors = {};
AlbumColors.getColors = function() {};
```

We'll then reference this file in the :prod build, as follows:

```
:prod {:source-paths ["src-cljs"]
       :compiler
       {:optimizations :advanced
        :externs ["resources/externs.js"]
        :output-to "resources/public/js/gallery-cljs.js"}}
```

Now if we clean and recompile our ClojureScript everything should work as expected:

```
lein cljsbuild clean && lein cljsbuild once prod
```

The resulting script is weighing in at only around 150kB. It might seem large for what it's doing, but remember that it's also providing the complete Clojure-Script runtime. This is no worse than having to include jQuery or a similar JavaScript library when working with plain JavaScript code.

SQL Korma

Now that we've Clojurized our front end, let's look at doing the same to our model. Up to now we've been using clojure.java.jdbc and writing SQL queries by hand. SQL Korma is a native Clojure DSL that allows us to write the queries using Clojure.[8]

Korma provides a way to write composable queries using Clojure that are translated to the resulting SQL. Because the DSL mimics SQL structure, the resulting queries are efficient and human-readable. The first thing we need to do is include the Korma dependency in our project:

```
[korma "0.3.0-RC5"]
```

We can now remove the org.clojure/java.jdbc dependency, as Korma depends on it and will ensure that it's pulled into our project. To use Korma, we simply need to wrap our connection using defdb:

```
(defdb korma-db db)
```

---

8.   http://sqlkorma.com/

This will create a connection pool for your db spec using the c3p0 library.[9] The last-created pool is set as the default for all queries.

Korma uses entities to represent SQL tables. The entities represent the core building blocks of your queries. These entities are created by using the defentity macro. Let's create the entities for our users and images tables. The entity name should be the same as the table name.

```
(defentity users)
```

```
(defentity images)
```

Note that when only a single connection is specified the entities will use it implicitly. We can now rewrite our user query functions as follows:

picture-gallery-korma/src/picture_gallery/models/db.clj
```
(defn create-user [user]
  (insert users (values user)))

(defn get-user [id]
  (first (select users
                 (where {:id id})
                 (limit 1))))

(defn delete-user [id]
  (delete users (where {:id id})))

(defn add-image [userid name]
  (transaction
    (if (empty? (select images
                        (where {:userid userid :name name})
                        (limit 1)))
      (insert images (values {:userid userid :name name}))
      (throw
        (Exception. "you have already uploaded an image with the same name")))))

(defn images-by-user [userid]
  (select images (where {:userid userid})))
(defn delete-image [userid name]
  (delete images (where {:userid userid :name name})))

(defn get-gallery-previews []
  (exec-raw
    ["select * from
    (select *, row_number() over (partition by userid) as row_number from images)
    as rows where row_number = 1" []]
    :results))
```

---

9. http://sourceforge.net/projects/c3p0/

As you can see, Korma-style queries mimic the original SQL fairly closely, but they have less noise. Since they're written in plain Clojure, we can manipulate them just like any other Clojure code.

The functions for adding, selecting, and deleting images are all easily translated as well:

picture-gallery-korma/src/picture_gallery/models/db.clj
```clojure
(defn add-image [userid name]
  (transaction
    (if (empty? (select images
                        (where {:userid userid :name name})
                        (limit 1)))
      (insert images (values {:userid userid :name name}))
      (throw
        (Exception. "you have already uploaded an image with the same name")))))


(defn images-by-user [userid]
  (select images (where {:userid userid})))
(defn delete-image [userid name]
  (delete images (where {:userid userid :name name})))
```

So far so good, but the get-gallery-previews function uses a bit more intricate of a query that can't easily be translated to Korma. In a case like that, we can use the exec-raw helper and pass it the query directly, as we did when using clojure.java.jdbc:

picture-gallery-korma/src/picture_gallery/models/db.clj
```clojure
(defn get-gallery-previews []
  (exec-raw
    ["select * from
    (select *, row_number() over (partition by userid) as row_number from images)
    as rows where row_number = 1" []]
    :results))
```

You might have noticed that by default Korma produces some noisy logging. To fix this we need to include a log4j dependency and add a log configuration for Korma. We'll add the following in our project dependencies:

```clojure
[log4j "1.2.15"
  :exclusions [javax.mail/mail
               javax.jms/jms
               com.sun.jdmk/jmxtools
               com.sun.jmx/jmxri]]
```

Then, we'll place a log4j.xml configuration file under our project's resources directory. The file contents should look like this:

picture-gallery-korma/resources/log4j.xml
```xml
<?xml version="1.0" encoding="UTF-8" ?>
<!DOCTYPE log4j:configuration SYSTEM "log4j.dtd">

<log4j:configuration xmlns:log4j="http://jakarta.apache.org/log4j/">
  <logger name="com.mchange">
    <level value="WARN"/>
  </logger>
</log4j:configuration>
```

That's all there is to it; Korma will now handle our SQL queries and we can express the logic using the standard Clojure notation.

Creating Application Templates

Once we create a particular type of application, such as our picture-gallery app, we may want to write other similar applications that use the same structure. It would be nice to be able to create a skeleton application template that could be used for this task. This is precisely what we can do by creating Leiningen templates.

Throughout this book we've been using the *compojure-app* template when we created new projects. Here we'll cover how this template works and how to make templates of our own.[10]

Leiningen uses the lein-newnew plug-in for template creation. To create a new template we merely have to run lein new template <template name>.[11]

Let's look inside the *compojure-app* template project to see how it works. Since it's a Leiningen project, it contains the project.clj.

compojure-template/project.clj
```clojure
(defproject compojure-app/lein-template "0.3.9"
  :description "Compojure project template for Leiningen"
  :url "https://github.com/yogthos/compojure-template"
  :eval-in-leiningen true
  :license {:name "Eclipse Public License"
            :url "http://www.eclipse.org/legal/epl-v10.html"}
  :dependencies [[leinjacker "0.2.0"]])
```

It looks like a regular project file, except for the eval-in-leiningen key that prevents Leiningen from launching a separate process for the given project during the build time.

---

10. https://github.com/yogthos/compojure-template
11. https://github.com/Raynes/lein-newnew

The template itself is found at src/compojure-template/leiningen/new/compojure_app.clj, and it looks like this:

```
compojure-template/src/leiningen/new/compojure_app.clj
(ns leiningen.new.compojure-app
  (:use [leiningen.new.templates :only [renderer sanitize year ->files]]
        [leinjacker.utils :only [lein-generation]]))

(defn check-lein-version []
  (if (< (lein-generation) 2)
    (throw (new Exception "Leiningen v2 is required..."))))

(defn compojure-app
  "Create a new Compojure project"
  [name]
  (check-lein-version)
  (let [data {:name name
              :sanitized (sanitize name)
              :year (year)}
        render #((renderer "compojure_app") % data)]
    (println "Generating a lovely new Compojure project named" (str name "..."))
    (->files data
             [".gitignore"  (render "gitignore")]
             ["project.clj" (render "project.clj")]
             ["README.md"    (render "README.md")]
             ["src/{{sanitized}}/repl.clj"         (render "repl.clj")]
             ["src/{{sanitized}}/handler.clj"      (render "handler.clj")]
             ["src/{{sanitized}}/routes/home.clj"  (render "home.clj")]
             ["src/{{sanitized}}/views/layout.clj" (render "layout.clj")]
             ["resources/public/css/screen.css"    (render "screen.css")]
             "resources/public/js"
             "resources/public/img"
             "src/{{sanitized}}/models"
             ["test/{{sanitized}}/test/handler.clj" (render "handler_test.clj")])))
```

The compojure-app function is where all the fun happens, and it's what gets called when we run lein new compojure-app myapp to create an application using this template.

The code in the template is mostly self-explanatory. It uses the leiningen.new.templates/render function to put the template files at the specified path. The {{sanitized}} tag ensures that the generated names for the package folders are valid, converting the dashes to underscores.

We find the template files themselves at the src/compojure-template/leiningen/new/compojure_app path. These files don't need to have the same folder structure as the resulting project. As you can see in the preceding code, we specify the target path explicitly in our template.

The templates are just regular files that would be found in the resulting project. The only difference is that they use the {{name}} anchor whenever the project name would be referenced. This anchor will be replaced with the name of the application that we specify when creating the project. Let's look at the layout.clj template as an example:

```
compojure-template/src/leiningen/new/compojure_app/layout.clj
(ns {{name}}.views.layout
  (:require [hiccup.page :refer [html5 include-css]]))
(defn common [& body]
  (html5
    [:head
     [:title "Welcome to {{name}}"]
     (include-css "/css/screen.css")]
    [:body body]))
```

Once we've created our template, we can install it locally by running lein install. Then we can start using it instead of having to write the boilerplate for this kind of project. If we wish to make our template available to others, we can publish it to Clojars by running lein deploy clojars.

What You've Learned

In this chapter we saw several approaches to structuring the application. We discussed how to plug in a different templating engine. We discussed how we're able to use Clojure on both the server and the client. Finally, we covered how to use the Korma DSL to access the database using Clojure syntax. As you probably noticed, we can have as much or as little Clojure as we want in our application.

At one extreme we could use Hiccup, ClojureScript, and Korma. This type of application would be written almost entirely in Clojure. The primary benefit of this approach is that we can do everything uniformly in one language. We don't need to remember syntax quirks of SQL and JavaScript, nor do we need to write any HTML by hand. The obvious downside to this approach is that we're able to work with only people versed in Clojure.

At the other extreme we have Selmer, JavaScript, and the clojure.java.jdbc library. Here, Clojure is used only for the application's business logic. This approach minimizes the impact of using Clojure. Most importantly, it allows us to work with people who aren't familiar with the language, such as DBAs and designers, as well as easily use powerful JavaScript frameworks such as AngularJs.[12]

---

12. http://angularjs.org/

Having a range of options available provides the flexibility to use Clojure for a wide variety of projects. More importantly, these options allow you to start using as much Clojure as you're comfortable with.

The Luminus Framework

The Clojure community eschews traditional-style frameworks, preferring composable libraries instead. The question is how you identify what libraries to use. Which work well together and are well maintained? If you're a professional you probably don't have a lot of time to discover this through trial and error.

While I agree that frameworks in a traditional sense don't add much value, I think there is certainly a need for having sets of curated libraries and standard patterns for doing things. Not only does this make it easier to start a project, but it also simplifies working on other projects that follow the same patterns.

You probably also noticed that there's some boilerplate involved in creating the applications. You have to set up the database, create a handler, add the relevant middleware, and so on.

Luminus aims to handle these things for you so you can focus on writing the core of your application.[13]

At its heart, Luminus is simply a Leiningen template that creates all the boilerplate for a typical web application. Unlike most templates, Luminus uses optional flags to set up a project using specific features. For example, we can use a +postgres flag to add support for the Postgres database, or a +cljs flag to include support for ClojureScript.

If we were building an application similar to our picture gallery, we could create a new application using the following flags:

```
lein new luminus picture-gallery +postgres +cljs
```

This would create an application set up to use the Postgres database, including the ClojureScript hooks. We'd simply have to add the code that's relevant to the application.

Final Words

This concludes our whirlwind tour of developing web applications with Clojure. We covered a wide range of topics, including development tools, libraries, configuration, and deployment. My hope is that by reading this text you'll

---

13. http://www.luminusweb.net/

have the necessary background to research the topics that we haven't covered as the need arises.

Some of the choices for the tools, libraries, and development practices discussed reflect the author's personal experience and preferences building web applications. In many cases there are other options available that are equally viable. Again, the goal here is to provide you with a solid foundation so that you can discover these on your own.

I sincerely hope that you enjoyed reading this book and that it will inspire you to use Clojure for your next web application. Clojure is a young language, and many quality tools and libraries are available, as is a fantastic community.

Alternative IDE Options

Although this book introduces Light Table, you very well might prefer using a different editor for your project. The good news is that Leiningen projects are editor-agnostic. In this appendix we'll look at some of the most popular alternatives to Light Table.

Installing Eclipse

You can download Eclipse from the official site,[1] and we'll use the *Eclipse IDE for Java Developers* distribution, as it contains everything we'll need. Once you have Eclipse downloaded, simply unpack it and run the executable found in the Eclipse folder.

Eclipse has full support for working with Leiningen projects provided via the Counterclockwise plug-in.[2] This allows us to create projects and manage their dependencies without having to leave the integrated development environment (IDE).

Installing the Counterclockwise Plug-in

Counterclockwise is available via its official update URL.[3] To install the plug-in go to the help menu in Eclipse and select the Install New Software option. Once there, paste the update-site URL in the Work With box. Select Clojure Programming and click Finish. You will be asked to confirm the untrusted source. Do so and then restart Eclipse when prompted.

Although it's not strictly necessary, I would encourage you to enable the structural-editing mode for Clojure. In this mode, the editor will ensure that

---

1. http://www.eclipse.org/downloads/
2. http://code.google.com/p/counterclockwise/
3. http://ccw.cgrand.net/updatesite/

your parens are properly balanced. It may take a bit of getting used to, but I guarantee you'll find yourself much more productive in the end. To enable this mode, simply navigate to Preferences/Clojure/Editor and check off the Start Editors in Strict/Paredit Edit Mode option.

Eclipse Configuration

Eclipse uses the concept of perspectives and views to present its user interface. Each perspective is optimized for a particular task, such as development, debugging, or source control. Within a perspective we can add different views, such as an editor, a project browser, a code outline, and so forth.

The most useful perspective for Clojure development is the Java perspective. There we can add the Package Explorer, Outline, Namespace Browser, and Console views. To do so, simply navigate to Window/Show View in the menu and select the views mentioned earlier if they're not already shown.

The Package Explorer allows us to explore our projects and see their files and dependencies. Outline shows all the functions defined in the currently open namespace. The Namespace Browser is active only when a read-evaluate-print loop (REPL) is running, and it provides an overview of all the functions that have been loaded. The console allows us to see any output from our application that's written to the standard out and the standard error.

Installing Emacs

Emacs is probably the oldest IDE that's still actively used today. Being a mature project, it has lots of features and plug-ins available, many of which don't have counterparts in other IDEs. However, it also means that Emacs doesn't follow any of the common patterns since it predates them.

Emacs is available for all the major platforms and can be downloaded from the official site.[4] If you're using OS X, you may want to look at Aquamacs, which is customized for the Mac.[5]

Unlike in most editors, shortcuts in Emacs often consist of chains of commands. For example, if we want to open a file, we would first type Ctrl-x, which puts us in command mode, then Ctrl-f, which lets us search for a file to open. The common abbreviation for the preceding command is C-x - C-f, and this is the notation we'll use going forward.

---

4. http://www.gnu.org/software/emacs/
5. http://aquamacs.org/

Other commands are invoked by using the meta key—*M* for short. This key is usually `Alt` on Windows and Linux, and `Cmd` on OS X. For example, we can update the list of available packages by running `M-x package-refresh-contents`.

Once you have Emacs downloaded and running, you'll need to configure it, and to configure Emacs for use with Clojure you'll need to install some additional packages. The recommended approach is to create the init.el file in the ~/.emacs.d/ directory. We'll then add the initialization scripts to it. This way, if you move to a different machine, you can simply copy over your init file and not have to configure Emacs again.

We first need to initialize our package manager with the URL of the package repository. Let's create a new file by running `C-x - C-f` and specifying the path as ~/.emacs.d/init.el.

Then we add the following code to initialize the package manager:

```
(require 'package)
(add-to-list 'package-archives
             '("marmalade" . "http://marmalade-repo.org/packages/"))
(package-initialize)
```

We save the file using `C-x - C-s`. With the file saved, let's refresh our package listing by running `M-x package-refresh-contents`. Once this completes, the package listing should be up-to-date. We can now specify the packages we'd like to be installed by adding them to our init file:

```
(defvar my-packages '(clojure-mode
                      clojure-test-mode
                      nrepl))

(dolist (p my-packages)
  (when (not (package-installed-p p))
    (package-install p)))
```

Here we'll use the *clojure-mode* package to add Clojure editing support.[6] The *nREPL* package provides an Emacs client for the Clojure network REPL server.[7] It will allow us to connect to our Leiningen projects from Emacs.

Let's save again, and evaluate our buffer by running `M-x eval-buffer`. The new packages will be downloaded and installed. You may see some warnings during the process. This is nothing to worry about.

Let's see how to load up a REPL session for the guestbook project we created earlier. We can do this by following these steps:

---

6. https://github.com/clojure-emacs/clojure-mode
7. https://github.com/clojure-emacs/nrepl.el

1. Open a namespace in our project by running `C-x`-`C-f` and selecting guest-book/src/guestbook/repl.clj.

2. With the repl.clj buffer selected, run `M-x nrepl-jack-in` to start the REPL server for the project and connect to it.

3. Run `C-c`-`M-n` to switch the REPL namespace to our buffer's.

4. Finally, run `C-c`-`C-k` to evaluate the buffer.

If all went well, Emacs will now be connected to your project and you can start hacking on it. Finally, I recommend taking a look at the Emacs Prelude project for further enhancements to the default Emacs behavior.[8]

Alternatives

If you're not satisfied with either Eclipse or Emacs as your Clojure editor, check out these alternatives.

Cursive

Another promising alternative is Cursive,[9] a new IDE based on the IntelliJ platform. At the time of writing it's in beta, but already usable for many projects, especially if you're currently an IntelliJ user. It provides full structural editing, Leiningen dependency management, and REPL support via nREPL. The installation instructions are available on the official site.

VimClojure

If you're a Vim user, you may wish to check out VimClojure.[10] The plug-in supports many expected features, such as syntax highlighting, indentation, and code completion. The main drawback of VimClojure is its lack of support for structural editing.

---

8. https://github.com/bbatsov/prelude
9. http://cursiveclojure.com
10. https://bitbucket.org/kotarak/vimclojure

Clojure Primer

As there are numerous books already available for learning Clojure, I'll keep this overview short. Even if you're not familiar with Clojure, I hope you'll find that most of the code in this book is easy to follow. Instead of looking at syntax in depth, I'd like to briefly go over the way Clojure programs are structured and some of the unique aspects of the language.

At first glance Clojure code can look rather alien and you might even feel that it's more difficult to read than other languages. I assure you that Clojure code is not inherently more difficult to understand, and with a bit of practice you might even feel it's quite the opposite.

Most of the differences between the mainstream languages are simply syntactic sugar, and very little effort is needed to move between them. This is not the case with Clojure. Being a Lisp dialect, it comes from a different branch of languages and requires some practice before it becomes natural. Don't be discouraged if initially the code appears hard to read. This is because you're learning new concepts as opposed to memorizing slightly different syntax.

A Functional Perspective

Clojure is a functional language. This makes it extremely well positioned for writing modern applications. As the application grows it's imperative to be able to reason about parts of the application in isolation. It's equally important to have code that is testable and reusable.

Managing State

Functional languages are ideal for writing large applications because they eschew global state and favor immutability as the default. When the data is predominantly immutable we can easily reason about parts of the application in isolation.

Immutable data structures might sound like a strange idea at first. However, many of the benefits associated with functional languages are directly facilitated by them. Let's look at what makes these data structures such a powerful tool.

In most languages data can be passed around either by value or by reference. Passing data by value is safe since we know that any changes we make to the data will not have any effect outside the function. However, it's also prohibitively expensive in many cases, so any substantial amount of data is passed around by reference. This can make code very difficult to reason about, as you have to know all the places where a piece of data is referenced to update it safely.

Immutable data structures provide us with a third option. Every time a change is made to a data structure a new revision is created. The price we pay when altering the data is proportional to the size of the change. When a piece of data is no longer referenced it simply gets garbage-collected.

I would liken this to using garbage collection instead of manual memory management. This allows us to effectively "copy" data any time we make a change without having to worry about where it comes from or what the scope of our change will be. The language will take care of figuring out what parts of it can be cleaned up when they're no longer used.

Having such data structures facilitates writing pure functions. A pure function is simply a function that has no side effects. Given the same parameters, the function will always produce the same result. Since such functions can be reasoned about in isolation, it makes it easy to write large applications that are composed of individual self-contained components. This type of code is referred to as being referentially transparent.

Achieving Code Reuse

Object-oriented languages tend to have strong coupling between the data and the functions that operate on it. In this scenario we can't easily reuse methods written in one class when we have a similar problem that we need to solve in another.

This problem does not exist in a functional language because the logic and data are kept separate. The language provides a small set of common data structures such as lists, maps, and sets. All the functions operate on these data structures and when we come to a new problem, we can easily reuse any function we write.

Each function represents a certain transformation that we wish to apply to our data. When we need to solve a problem we simply have to understand the sequence of transformations and map those to the appropriate functions. This style of code is referred to as *declarative*.

Declarative code separates what is being done from how it is done. When we wish to iterate over a collection, we use an iterator function. The logic that we want to execute inside the iteration will be passed in as a parameter.

One important advantage of this style is that we benefit from having code reuse at the function level. An iterator function can be written once to handle the edge cases and boundary checks. Then we can reuse this logic without having to worry about remembering to do these checks time and again.

Leveraging Multiprocessing

Functional code also makes it easier to tackle the difficult problems of parallelism and concurrency. While there is no silver bullet for addressing either problem, the language can certainly make it easier to reason about them.

Since pure functions depend only on their arguments, they do not rely on any shared state and can safely be computed in parallel. This means we can easily parallelize many algorithms to take advantage of the extra cores. An example of this is mapping a function over the items in a collection. We can start by writing a version using the map function. Should we discover that each operation takes a significant amount of time, then we can simply switch to using pmap to run the operations in parallel.

Meanwhile, the immutable data structures provide an excellent tool for managing shared state. Clojure provides a Software Transactional Memory (STM) library based on these data structures. With transactional memory we no longer have to worry about manual locking when dealing with threads. Additionally, the data only needs to be locked for writing. Since the existing data is immutable, it can be read safely even while an update is happening.

Data Types

Clojure provides a number of data types, most of which are unsurprising:

- *Vars* provide mutable storage locations. These can be bound and rebound on a per-thread basis.

- *Booleans* can have a value of true or false; *nil* values are also treated as false.

- *Numbers* can be integers, doubles, floats, and fractions.

- *Symbols* are used as identifiers for variables.
- *Keywords* are symbols that reference themselves and are denoted by a colon; these are often used as keys in maps.
- *Strings* are denoted by double quotes and can span multiple lines.
- *Characters* are denoted by a forward slash.
- *Regular expressions* are strings prefixed with a hash symbol.

In addition to the data types, Clojure provides a rich set of standard collections. These include lists, vectors, maps, and sets.

- List: (1 2 3)
- Vector: [1 2 3]
- Map: {:foo "a" :bar "b"}
- Set: #{"a" "b" "c"}

Interestingly, Clojure code is written using the data structures you've just seen. This is very different from most languages, where you have one syntax for defining data and a separate syntax for writing the program logic. Using the same syntax for both allows for the powerful metaprogramming features.

You can manipulate any piece of Clojure code like any other data structure. This provides an easy way to create templates for recurring patterns in your problem domain.

Using Functions

Function calls in Clojure look very similar to those in other languages. Let's look at calling a function in Python and in Clojure:

```
functionName(param1, param2)
```

```
(function-name param1 param2)
```

The main difference is that the function name comes after the paren in the Clojure version. This is because a function call is simply a list containing the function name and its parameters. A list is a special data structure in Clojure because the compiler expects the first argument in lists to be callable. If you wanted to create a list data structure, you'd call the list function.

```
(list 1 2 3)
```

Anonymous Functions

Clojure allows creation of functions without having to name them. Such functions are referred to as *lambda expressions*. These functions can be defined by using the fn special form. A special form is a type of a primitive that is evaluated using different rules than the standard primitives. Each special form can have a unique way to evaluate its arguments.

For example, if we wanted a function that prints a single argument, we could write the following:

```
(fn [arg] (println arg))
```

We could then pass a parameter to this function to be printed.

```
((fn [arg] (println arg)) "hello")

=>"hello"
```

Clojure also provides syntactic sugar for defining anonymous functions using the # notation. The preceding function can be rewritten more concisely as follows:

```
#(println %)
```

Here, the % symbol indicates an unnamed argument. If the function accepted multiple arguments, then each one would be followed by a number indicating its position. This can be seen in the next example:

```
#(println %1 %2 %3)
```

The preceding anonymous function accepts three arguments and prints them out in order. This type of function is useful when you need to perform a one-off operation that doesn't warrant defining a named function. These functions are often used in conjunction with the higher-order functions, which we'll look at in a moment.

Named Functions

Named functions are simply anonymous functions bound to a symbol used as an identifier. Clojure provides a special form called def that's used for creating global variables. It accepts a name and the body to be assigned to it. We can create a named function by using def as follows:

```
(def double (fn ([x] (* 2 x))))
```

Since this is such a common operation, Clojure provides a special form called defn that does it for us:

```
(defn square [x]
  (* x x))
```

The first argument to defn is the name of the function being defined. It is followed by a vector containing the arguments and the body of the function. In the preceding code, we passed in a single item for the body; however, we could pass as many items as we like:

```
(defn bar [a b]
  (println a)
  (println b)
  (* 2 (+ a b)))
```

Here we define the function bar that takes parameters a and b. The body consists of two print statements and a call to sum a and b then multiply the result by 2. All the expressions are evaluated from the inside out. In the last statement, (+ a b) is evaluated, then its result is multiplied by two and returned by bar.

One thing to note is that Clojure uses a single pass compiler. For this reason, the functions must be declared before they are used. In a case when we need to refer to a function before it's been defined, we must use the declare macro to provide a forward declaration.

```
(declare down)
```

```
(defn up [n]
  (if (< n 10)
    (down (+ 2 n))
    n))
```

```
(defn down [n]
  (up (dec n)))
```

As you might have noticed, the code structure is a tree. This tree is called the *abstract syntax tree*, or AST for short. This is the same AST that the compiler sees when compiling the code. By being able to see the AST directly, we can see the relationships between pieces of logic visually.

Since we write our code in terms of data, there are fewer syntactic hints than in most languages. For example, as you might have noticed, there are no explicit return statements. Instead, the last expression of the function body is returned implicitly. This might take a little getting used to if you're accustomed to seeing a lot of annotations in your code. To aid readability, functions are often kept short (five lines or less is a good rule of thumb) while indentation and spacing are used for grouping code visually.

In Clojure, there is no distinction between functions and variables. You can assign a function to a label, pass it as a parameter, or return a function from another function. Functions that can be treated as data are referred to as being *first-class* because they don't have any additional restrictions attached to them.

Higher-Order Functions

Functions that take other functions as parameters are called higher-order functions. One example of such a function is map:

```
(map #(* % %) [1 2 3 4 5])
=>(1 4 9 16 25)
```

Here we pass in two parameters to map. The first parameter is an anonymous function that squares its argument and the second is a collection of numbers. The map function will visit each item in the collection and square it. One advantage of using higher-order functions is that we don't have to worry about boundary conditions, such as nil checks. The iterator function handles these for us.

Another example of a higher-order function is filter. This function goes through a collection and keeps only the items matching the condition specified.

```
(filter even? [1 2 3 4 5])
=>(2 4)
```

You can, of course, chain these functions together to solve problems:

```
(filter even?
  (map #(* 3 %) [1 2 3 4 5]))
=>(6 12)
```

Here we multiply each item by 3, then we use filter to only keep the even items from the resulting sequence.

Because of higher-order functions, you should practically never have to write loops or explicit recursion. When you need to iterate a collection, use a function such as map or filter instead. Since Clojure has a rich standard library, practically any data transformation can be achieved by a combination of several higher-order functions.

Instead of having to learn a lot of different language features and syntax, you simply have to learn the functions in the standard library. Once you learn to associate data transformations with specific functions, many problems can be solved by simply putting existing functions together.

Here is a real-world example of this idea. The problem is to display a formatted address given the fields representing it. Commonly an address has a unit number, a street, a city, a postal code, and a country. We'll have to examine each of these pieces, remove the null and empty ones, and insert some separator between them.

Let's say we have a table in our database that contains the following fields:

```
unit       | street            | city     | postal_code | country
""         | "1 Main street"   | Toronto  | nil         | Canada
```

Given the preceding data as strings, we would like to output the following formatted string:

```
1 Main street, Toronto, Canada
```

All we have to do is find the functions for the tasks of removing empty fields, interposing the separator, and concatenating the result into a string:

```
(defn concat-fields [& fields]
  (apply str (interpose ", " (remove empty? fields))))
```

```
(concat-fields "" "1 Main street" "Toronto" nil "Canada")
 =>"1 Main street, Toronto, Canada"
```

Notice that we didn't have to specify how to do any of the tasks when writing our code. Much of the time we simply say what we're doing by composing the functions representing the operations we wish to carry out.

Closures

Next we'll look at functions that return other functions as a result. One use for such functions is to provide behavior that is facilitated by constructors in object-oriented languages. For example, if you want to initialize some variables before using a function, you can do so as follows:

```
(defn make-client [url]
  (fn [request] (str "sending " request " to " url)))
(let [client (make-client "http://foo.org")]
  (println (client "request 1"))
  (println (client "request 2")))
```

Here we create a function that accepts a url parameter and returns a function that accepts a request as its parameter. The inner function has access to the url variable since it's defined in the same scope.

This type of function is called a *closure* because it closes over its parameters, in our case the url, and makes them available to the functions it returns.

You'll notice that we're using a form called let to bind the client symbol. This makes it available to any expressions inside the let form. The let form serves the same purpose as declaring variables in imperative languages.

Threading Expressions

As you might suspect by now, expressions can become difficult to read if they're deeply nested. Luckily for us, Clojure provides a couple of helper forms to address this problem. Let's say we have a range of ten numbers, and we want to increment each number, interpose the number 5 between them, then sum the result. We could write the following:

```
(reduce + (interpose 5 (map inc (range 10))))
```

It's a little difficult to tell what's happening in that expression at first glance. If each step were even a little more complex, we'd be really lost. On top of that, if we wanted to rearrange any of the steps, such as interposing 5 before incrementing, then we'd have to renest all our expressions.

An alternative way to write the preceding is to use the ->> form:

```
(->> (range 10) (map inc) (interpose 5) (reduce +))
```

Here, we use the ->> to *thread* the operations from one to another. This means we implicitly pass the result of each expression as the *last* argument of the next expression. If we wanted to pass it as the *first* argument instead, we could use the -> form to do that.

Being Lazy

Many Clojure algorithms use lazy evaluation. This means the operations aren't performed unless somebody actually asks for their result. This is crucial to making many algorithms work efficiently.

For example, you might think the preceding example is very inefficient since we have to iterate our sequence each time to create the range, map across it, interpose, and reduce the result.

However, this is not actually the case. The evaluation of each expression happens on demand. The first value in range is generated and passed to the rest of the functions, then the next, and so on, until the sequence is exhausted. This is similar to the way *iterators* work in languages like Python.

Structuring the Code

One nontrivial difference between Clojure and most other languages is the way that the code is structured. In imperative languages, a common practice is for different lines of code to modify shared data, where each line accessing the memory location sees the result of the previous line of code.

For example, if we have a list of integers and we wish to square each one then print the even ones, the following Python code would be perfectly valid:

```
l = [1, 2, 3, 4, 5]
for i in l
  i = i*i

for i in l
 if (i mod 2 == 0)

print l
```

In Clojure this interaction is explicit. Instead of creating a shared memory location and then having different functions access it sequentially, we chain functions together and pipe the input through them:

```
(println
  (filter #(= (mod % 2) 0)
    (map #(* % %) (range 1 6)))))
```

Or, as we've covered, we could use the ->> macro to flatten the operations:

```
(->> (range 1 6)
     (map #(* % %))
     (filter #(= (mod % 2) 0))
     (println))
```

Each function returns a new value instead of modifying the existing data in place. You might think that this can get very expensive, and it would with a naïve implementation where the entirety of the data is copied with every change.

In reality, Clojure is backed by persistent data structures that create in-memory revisions of the data.[1] Each time a change is made a new revision is created proportional to the size of the change. With this approach we only pay the price of the difference between the old and the new data structures while ensuring that any changes are inherently localized.

Destructuring Data

Clojure has a powerful mechanism called destructuring for declaratively accessing values in data structures. If you know the data structure's type, you can describe it using a literal notation in the binding. Let's look at some examples of what this means.

```
(let [[smaller bigger] (split-with #(< % 5) (range 10))]
  (println smaller bigger))

=>(0 1 2 3 4) (5 6 7 8 9)
```

---

1.   http://en.wikipedia.org/wiki/Persistent_data_structure

Here we use split-with to split a range of ten numbers into a sequence containing two elements: numbers less than 5 and numbers greater than or equal to 5. The split-with function returns a sequence containing two elements: the first is the sequence of items that are less than 5, and the other is the ones that are greater. Since we know the result's format, we can write it in a literal form as [smaller bigger], and then use these named elements within the let binding.

We can use this type of destructuring in function definitions as well. Next we have a function called print-user that accepts a vector with three items. It names the items name, address, and phone, respectively.

```
(defn print-user [[name address phone]]
  (println name address phone))
```

```
(print-user ["Bob" "12 Jarvis street, Toronto" "416-987-3417"])
```

We can also specify variable arguments as a sequence in cases where a variable number of arguments can be supplied. This is done by using the ampersand followed by the name for the argument list.

```
(defn foo [& args]
  (println args))
```

```
(foo "a" "b" "c")
=>(a b c)
```

Since the variable arguments are stored in a sequence, we can use destructuring with them as well.

```
(defn foo [first-arg & [second-arg]]
  (println (if second-arg
             "two arguments were passed in"
             "one argument was passed in")))
(foo "bar")
=>"one argument was passed in"
```

```
(foo "bar" "baz")
=>"two arguments were passed in"
```

We can also use destructuring with maps. When destructuring a map, we create a map with names bound locally to the keys from the original map:

```
(let [{foo :foo bar :bar} {:foo "foo" :bar "bar"}]
  (println foo bar)
```

It's possible to destructure a nested data structure, as well. As long as you know the data's structure, you can simply write it out.

```
(let [{[a b c] :items id :id} {:id "foo" :items [1 2 3]}]
  (println id " has the following items " a b c))
```

Finally, there is some syntactic sugar for extracting keys from maps, as it's a common operation. For example, if we have a map containing the keys :id and :password, we could write a login function that would extract these keys in its definition.

```
(defn login [{:keys [id password]}]
  ...)
(login {:id "bob" :password "secret"})
```

Sometimes we'd like to extract some keys, but also have the original map available to us.

```
(defn [{:keys [id pass pass1] :as user}]
  (if (and id (= pass pass1))
    (println "valid user")
    (println user " is not filled in correctly")))
```

Namespaces

When writing real-world applications we need the tools to organize our code into logical groups. In object-oriented languages it's common to use classes and define methods as members of a class. In Clojure, we group our functions into namespaces instead. Let's look at how a namespace is defined.

```
(ns myns)

(defn print-message [message]
  (println "message:" message))

(defn say-hello [user]
  (print-message (str "hello " user)))
```

Here we have a namespace called myns containing two functions, print-message and say-hello. The functions in the same namespace can call each other directly. However, if we wanted to call these functions from a different namespace we would have to reference the myns first in the declaration of that namespace.

There are two ways of referencing a namespace in Clojure.

The :use Keyword

The first method is to reference the namespace by delcaring it with the :use keyword. When referenced in this way, all its Vars become implicitly available as if they were defined in the namespace that references it.

```
(ns myotherns
  (:use myns))
(say-hello "Bob")
```

There are two downsides to this approach. We don't know where the function was originally defined, making it difficult to navigate the code, and if we reference two namespaces that define the same name for a function, we'll get an error.

We can address the first problem by selecting the functions we wish to use explicitly using the :only keyword in our :use declaration.

```
(ns myotherns
 (:use [myns :only [say-hello]]))

(defn print-message [message]
 (println "in myotherns"))

(say-hello)
```

This way we document where say-hello comes from, and we're able to declare our own print-message in the myotherns namespace without conflicts. However, say-hello will still use the print-message defined in myns.

The :require Keyword

Another approach is to reference the namespace using the :require keyword. The :require keyword allows for using multiple strategies. Let's look at each of these.

We can require a namespace without providing any further directives. In this case, any calls to Vars inside it must be prefixed with the namespace declaration indicating their origin.

```
(ns myotherns
 (:require myns))

(myns/say-hello)
```

This approach is explicit about the origin of the Vars being referenced and ensures that we won't have conflicts when referencing multiple namespaces. One problem is that if our namespace declaration is long, it gets tedious to have to type it out any time we wish to use a function declared inside it. To alleviate this problem, the :require statement supports the :as directive, allowing us to create an alias for the namespace.

```
(ns myotherns
 (:require [myns :as m]))

(m/say-hello)
```

We can also require functions from a namespace by using the :refer keyword. This is synonymous with the :use notation we saw earlier.

To require all the functions from another namespace, we can write the following:

```
(ns myotherns
 (:require [myns :refer :all]))
```

If we wish to select what functions to require by name, we can instead write this:

```
(ns myotherns
 (:require [myns :refer [say-hello]]))
```

As you can see, there's a number of options available for referencing Vars declared in other namespaces. If you're not sure what option to pick, then requiring the namespace by name or alias is the safest route.

Dynamic Variables

Clojure provides support for declaring dynamic variables that can have their value changed within a particular scope. Let's look at how this works.

```
(declare ^{:dynamic true} *foo*)
(println *foo*)
=>#<Unbound Unbound: #'bar/*foo*>
```

Here we declared *foo* as a dynamic Var and didn't provide any value for it. When we try to print *foo* we get an error indicating that this Var has not been bound to any value.

Let's look at how we can assign a value to *foo* using a binding.

```
(defn with-foo [f]
  (binding [*foo* "foo"]
    (f)))
(with-foo #(println *foo*))
=>foo
```

We set *foo* to a string with value "foo" inside our with-foo function. When our anonymous function is called inside with-foo we no longer get an error when trying to print its value.

This technique can be useful when dealing with resources such as file streams, database connections, or scoped variables. In general, the use of dynamic variables is discouraged since they make code more opaque and difficult to reason about. However, there are legitimate uses for them, and it's worth knowing how they work.

Calling Out to Java

One advantage of using Clojure is that we can rely on the rich ecosystem of existing Java libraries. If some functionality is not available natively, we may wish to call out to a Java library to accomplish a particular task. Calling Java classes is very simple, and follows the standard Clojure syntax fairly closely.

Importing Classes

When we wish to use a Clojure library, we employ :use and :require statements. However, when we wish to import a Java class, we have to use the :import statement.

```
(ns myns
  (:import java.io.File))
```

We can also group multiple classes from the same package in a single import, as follows:

```
(ns myns
  (:import [java.io File FileInputStream FileOutputStream]))
```

Instantiating Classes

To create an instance of a class, we can call new just as we would in Java.

```
(new File ".")
```

There is also a commonly used shorthand for creating new objects:

```
(File. ".")
```

Calling Methods

Once we have an instance of a class, we can call methods on it. The notation is similar to making a regular function call. When we call a method, we pass the object its first parameter followed by any other parameters that the method accepts.

```
(let [f (File. ".")]
  (println (.getAbsolutePath f)))
```

There, we created a new file object f, and we called .getAbsolutePath on it. Notice that methods have a period (.) in front of them to differentiate them from regular Clojure functions. If we wanted to call a static function or a variable in a class, we would use the / notation, as follows.

```
(str File/separator "foo" File/separator "bar")
```

```
(Math/sqrt 256)
```

There's also a shorthand for chaining multiple method calls together using the double period (..) notation. Say we wanted to get the string indicating the file path and then get its bytes; we could write the code for that in two ways.

```
(.getBytes (.getAbsolutePath (File. ".")))
```

```
(.. (File. ".") getAbsolutePath getBytes)
```

The second notation looks more natural and easier to read. Although there is other syntactic sugar for working with Java, the preceding is sufficient for following the material we cover in this book.

Dynamic Polymorphism

Protocols allow defining an abstract set of functions that can be implemented by a concrete type. Let's look at an example protocol:

```
(defprotocol Foo
  "Foo doc string"
  (bar [this b] "bar doc string")
  (baz [this] [this b] "baz doc string"))
```

As you can see, the Foo protocol specifies two methods, bar and baz. The first argument to the method will be the object instance followed by its parameters. Note that the baz method has multiple arity. We can now create a type that implements the Foo protocol using the deftype macro:

```
(deftype Bar [data]
  Foo
  (bar [this param] (println data param))
  (baz [this] (println (class this)))
  (baz [this param] (println param)))
```

There we create type Bar that implements protocol Foo. Each method will print out some of its parameters. Let's see what it looks like when we create an instance of Bar and call its methods:

```
(let [b (Bar. "some data")]
  (.bar b "param")
  (.baz b)
  (.baz b "baz with param"))
```

```
some data param
Bar
baz with param
```

The first method call prints out the data Bar was initialized with and the parameter that was passed in. The second method call prints out the object's class, while the last method call demonstrates the other arity of baz.

We can also use protocols to extend the functionality of existing types, including existing Java classes. For example, we can use extend-protocol to extend the java.lang.String class with the Foo protocol:

```
(extend-protocol Foo
  String
  (bar [this param] (println this param)))
(bar "hello" "world")

hello world
```

For the purposes of this text the preceding examples will suffice. However, there are many other uses for protocols and I encourage you to take the time to discover them on your own.

What about Global State?

While predominantly immutable, Clojure provides support for shared mutable data as well via its STM library.[2] The STM ensures that all updates to mutable variables are done atomically. There are two major kinds of mutable types: the atom and the ref. The atom is used in cases where we need to do uncoordinated updates and the ref is used when we might need to do multiple updates as a transaction.

Let's look at an example of defining an atom and using it.

```
(def global-val (atom nil))
```

We've defined an atom called global-val and its current value is nil. We can now read its value by using the deref function, which returns the current value.

```
(println (deref global-val))
=>nil
```

Since this is a common operation, there is a shorthand for deref: the @ symbol. So writing (println @global-val) is equivalent to the preceding.

Let's look at two ways of setting a new value for our atom. We can either use reset! and pass in the new value, or we can use swap! and pass in a function that accepts the current value and updates it.

```
(reset! global-val 10)
(println @global-val)
=>10
(swap! global-val inc)
(println @global-val)
=>11
```

---

2. http://clojure.org/concurrent_programming

Note that both swap! and reset! end in an exclamation point (!); this is a convention to indicate that these functions operate on mutable data.

We define refs the same way we define atoms, but the two are used rather differently. Let's take a quick look at how they work.

```
(def names (ref []))

(dosync
  (ref-set names ["John"])
  (alter names #(if (not-empty %)
                  (conj % "Jane") %)))
```

In that code, we define a ref called names, then open a transaction using a dosync statement. Inside the transaction we set the names to a vector with the value "John". Next, we call alter to check if names is not empty and add "Jane" to the vector of names if that's the case.

Note that since this is happening inside a transaction, the check for emptiness depends on the existing state along with any state built up within the same transaction. If we tried to add or remove a name in a different transaction, it would have no visible effect on ours. However, one of the transactions would end up being retried.

Writing Code That Writes Code for You

Clojure, being a Lisp, also provides a powerful macro system. Macros allow templating repetitive blocks of code and deferring evaluation, among numerous other uses. A macro works by treating code as data instead of evaluating it. This allows us to manipulate the code tree just like any other data structure.

Macros execute before compile time and the compiler sees whatever the result of executing the macro will be. Because of this level of indirection, macros can be difficult to reason about, and thus it's best not to use them when a function will do the job.

However, there are legitimate uses for macros, and it's worth understanding how they work. In this book we use very few macros, so we'll only touch on their syntax superficially.

Let's look at a concrete example of a macro and see how it differs from the regular code we saw previously. Let's imagine that we have a session that will contain a user if one logs in. We might want to load certain content only if a user is present in the session.

```
(def session (atom {:user "Bob"}))

(defn load-content []
  (if (:user @session)
    "some content"
    "please log in"))
```

This will work, but it's tedious and error-prone to write our if statement every single time. Since our condition's logic stays the same, we can template this function as follows:

```
(defmacro defprivate [name & body]
  `(defn ~(symbol name) []
     (if (:user @session)
       (do ~@body)
       "please log in")))
```

The macros are defined using the defmacro special form. The major difference between defn and defmacro is that the parameters passed to defmacro are not evaluated by default.

To evaluate the parameter we use the tilde, as we're doing with ~(symbol name). Using the ~ notation indicates that we'd like to replace the name with the value it refers to. This is called *unquoting*.

The ~@ notation used in (do ~@body) is called *unquote splicing*. This notation is used when we're dealing with a sequence. The contents of the sequence will be merged into the outer form during the splicing. In this case body consists of a list representing the function's body. The body must be wrapped in a do block because the if statement requires having no more than two arguments.

The backtick (`) sign means that we wish to treat the following list as data instead of executing it. This is the opposite of unquoting, and it's referred to as *syntax-quoting*.

As I mentioned earlier, the macros are executed before compile time. To see what the macro will be rewritten as when the compiler sees it, we can call macroexpand-1.

```
(macroexpand-1 '(defprivate foo (println "bar")))
```

```
(clojure.core/defn foo []
  (if (:user (clojure.core/deref user/session))
    (do (println "bar"))
    "please log in"))
```

You can see that (defprivate foo (println "bar")) gets rewritten with a function definition that has the if statement inside. This resulting code is what the compiler will see, and it's equivalent to what we would have to write by hand otherwise. Now we can simply define a private function using our macro, and it will do the check for us automatically.

```
(defprivate foo (println "bar"))
```

The preceding example might seem a little contrived, but it demonstrates the power of being able to easily template repetitions in code. This allows creating a notation that expresses your problem domain using the language that is natural to it.

The Read-Evaluate-Print Loop

Another big aspect of working in Clojure is the read-evaluate-print loop (REPL). In many languages you write the code, then run the entire program to see what it does. In Clojure most development is done interactively using the REPL. In this mode we can see each piece of code we write in action as soon as it's written.

In nontrivial applications it's often necessary to build up a particular state before you can add more functionality. For example, a user has to log in and query some data from a back end, then you need to write functions to format and display this data. With a REPL you can get the application to the state where the data is loaded and then write the display logic interactively without having to reload the application and build up the state every time you make a change.

I find this method of development satisfying because of the immediate feedback from the application when you add or modify code. You can easily try things out and see how they work. It encourages experimentation and refactoring code as you go, which in turn helps you to write better and cleaner code.

Summary

This concludes our tour of Clojure basics. Although we touched on only a small portion of the overall language, if you understand the preceding examples then you should have no trouble following any of the code in the rest of the book. Once you have your development environment up and running, don't hesitate to try out the examples shown here in the REPL and play around with them until you feel comfortable moving on.

APPENDIX 3

Document-Oriented Database Access

A SQL database may not always be a good fit for your application. Many applications do not require a relational schema. If the application simply needs a persistence layer to store and retrieve records, then a document store may be a good fit.

Picking the Right Database

There are three main aspects to consider when picking a document-based database. These are consistency, availability, and partition tolerance, as defined by the CAP theorem.[1] Since these goals are at odds with each other, when picking the data store you'll have to decide which two are most important to you.

Consistency

When we have consistency, each client has the same view of the data. This aspect comes into play when you have a database cluster with multiple nodes. In a consistent database, each node is guaranteed to have the same view of the data.

Some databases, such as CouchDB,[2] provide eventual consistency. This means that while each node in the cluster is self-consistent, it's not guaranteed to be serving up the latest data.

Availability

Availability means there's no global lock on the database. A client connected to any node can read and write freely. However, the data is guaranteed to

---

1. http://en.wikipedia.org/wiki/CAP_theorem
2. http://couchdb.apache.org/

propagate through the cluster eventually. The downside of this approach is that clients are not guaranteed to see the latest data at all times.

CouchDB uses this model to allow high-availability clustering. Note that the clusters should always have an odd number of nodes. This allows CouchDB to use a quorum to decide what record will be kept in case of a conflict. Such a scenario can occur if two clients are updating a record while connected to different nodes. One of the clients will end up with a revision conflict in this scenario.

Partition Tolerance

A partition-tolerant database works well across physical network partitions. This means that even if your cluster experiences a serious network outage, the nodes will be able to resync automatically when the network becomes available.

Using CouchDB

CouchDB values availability and partition tolerance. This makes it ideal for creating clusters where you want high throughput without a bottleneck.

In this section we'll cover how to use CouchDB from Clojure to accomplish basic tasks such as storing, retrieving, and deleting documents.

As a prerequisite to working with the following examples, you'll need to either set up a local instance of CouchDB or use one of the free CouchDB services, such as Iris Couch.[3] Once you have the database set up, create a new table using its web user interface, accessible at http://hostname:5984/_utils. We'll call this table clutchtest.

Clutch Library

The easiest way to access CouchDB from Clojure is to use the Clutch library.[4] Clutch provides a very simple and intuitive interface. To use the library we must first add its dependency to our project. The latest version at the time of writing is [com.ashafa/clutch "0.4.0-RC1""].

Connecting to the Database

To use clutch, we must require it in our namespace declaration.

```
(:require [com.ashafa.clutch :as couch])
```

---

3. http://www.iriscouch.com/
4. https://github.com/clojure-clutch/clutch

Then we have to define our connection URL. Since CouchDB is accessible over HTTP, our URL can be a simple string specifying the database address.

```
(def db "http://localhost:5984/clutchtest")
```

We could also add authentication to the URL directly in our connection string.

```
(def db "http://user:pass@localhost:5984/clutchtest")
```

Or we could use the URL library to create a URL and attach the credentials to it as a map.[5]

```
(def db (assoc (cemerick.url/url "https://localhost:5984/" "clutchtest")
                :username "user"
                :password "pass"))
```

Now that we have the connection created, let's look at how to store documents in our database.

Storing Documents

All interaction with the database must happen inside the with-db macro. This macro ensures that the connection is closed properly after we're done.

To store a document in the database, we can call the put-document function and pass it a Clojure map representing our document.

```
(couch/with-db db
  (couch/put-document {:foo "bar"}))
```

The preceding will create a new document in our database with a randomly generated ID assigned to it. To assign a specific ID to a document, we must include the :_id key in our map.

```
(couch/with-db db
  (couch/put-document
    {:_id "user" :username "foo" :pass "$dfsdf#23434"}))
```

When we wish to update an existing document, we must also include the revision of the current document in the map. For example, if we already inserted a user document into our database, we must now specify the revision we're updating using the :_rev key:

```
(couch/with-db db
  (couch/put-document
    {:_id "user" :_rev "<revision number>" :username "foo" :pass "$dfsdf#23434"}))
```

---

5.   https://github.com/cemerick/url

When we retrieve a document from the database it will have both the :_id and :_rev keys populated, so make sure to preserve them for when you wish to save the document again. Now let's look at how we get a document from the database.

Retrieving a Single Document

Documents are retrieved using the get-document function, which accepts a string representing the ID of the document being retrieved.

```
(couch/with-db db
  (couch/get-document "user"))
```

We can, of course, combine multiple statements inside a single with-db statement. For example, if we wanted to retrieve the user, set a new username, and save the document, we could do the following:

```
(couch/with-db db
  (let [doc (couch/get-document "user")]
    (couch/put-document
      (assoc doc :username "bar")))
  (println (couch/get-document "user")))
```

Retrieving Multiple Documents

Sometimes we need to do a batch operation to retrieve multiple documents from the database. Clutch provides a function for doing this, called all-documents.

```
(couch/with-db db
  (couch/all-documents))
```

The preceding call returns the IDs and revisions for all the documents in the specified database. It is also possible to retrieve the complete documents from the database by setting the :include_docs key to true.

```
(couch/with-db db
  (couch/all-documents {:include_docs true}))
```

Additionally, we can restrict the bulk retrieval to a set of documents containing the IDs specified by the :keys keyword, as follows:

```
(couch/with-db db
  (couch/all-documents
    {:include_docs true}
    {:keys ["doc1" "doc2" "doc3"]}))
```

To do more-complex selections from CouchDB, you would typically create views to filter and return documents based on the application's needs. A view is analogous to a stored procedure in a relational database.

Deleting Documents

Finally, we delete documents by using the delete-document function. It accepts the document ID as a string and removes that document from the database.

```
(couch/with-db db
  (couch/delete-document "user"))
```

That's all there is to it when using CouchDB from Clojure. Clutch makes it trivial to store and retrieve documents from the database, and more-complex functionality can be added to the database directly via its rich-views support. Now let's look at what's involved in accessing MongoDB using the Monger library.[6,7]

Using MongoDB

MongoDB is another popular document-oriented database. Unlike CouchDB, it favors consistency and partition tolerance as its primary goals. If you're not concerned with having global locks, then MongoDB is an excellent choice.

Connecting to the Database

We'll use the Monger library for accessing MongoDB. Monger provides an idiomatic Clojure application programming interface for working with the database. It provides comprehensive support for the features MongoDB 2.2+ offers. As is the case with Clutch, we can use native Clojure data structures without having to worry about translating them into the MongoDB/BSON format. Finally, Monger defaults to configuration that emphasizes safety and consistency.

Connecting to the database is as easy as calling monger.core/connect!. When supplied no parameters, connect! will attempt to connect to a local instance of the database using the default port. Alternatively, we can either provide a map with the :host and :port keys, or fine-tune the connection using mongo-options. Let's see how this looks:

```
(ns mongo-example.core
  (:require [monger.core :as m])
  (:import
    org.bson.types.ObjectId
    [com.mongodb MongoOptions]))

;;connects to a local instance
(m/connect!)
```

---

6.   http://www.mongodb.org/
7.   http://clojuremongodb.info/

```
;;connect to myhost.com on port 5001
(m/connect! {:host "myhost.com" :port 5001})

;;connect using custom options
(m/connect! (m/server-address "127.0.0.1" 27017)
            (m/mongo-options
              :threads-allowed-to-block-for-connection-multiplier 300))
```

We can also set the default database using the *mongodb-database* Var by calling the set-db! function, as follows:

```
(defn connect! [& [params]]
  ((partial monger.core/connect!) params)
  (monger.core/set-db! (monger.core/get-db "local")))
```

Setting the database with set-db! makes it implicitly available to subsequent queries.

Most of the interaction with the database is provided via the monger.collection namespace. Here we have functions to insert, select, update, and delete records. Let's look at each of these tasks:

Inserting Records

We use the insert function to insert new records in the database. The function accepts the name of the collection, denoted by a string and a map representing the document to be inserted.

```
(monger.collection/insert "users" { :first_name "John" :last_name "Doe" })
```

The function returns a write result, the status of which can be checked by using monger.result/ok?. The monger.result/ok? will return true if the write was successful.

If we wish to specify an ID for our document, we have to generate it using the org.bson.types.ObjectId:

```
(monger.collection/insert "users" { :first_name "John" :last_name "Doe" })

(monger.collection/insert
  "users"
  { :_id (ObjectId.) :first_name "John" :last_name "Doe" })
```

Next, we have the insert-and-return function. It acts exactly like insert, except it returns the inserted document as a map.

```
(monger.collection/insert-and-return "users"
  { :_id (ObjectId.) :first_name "John" :last_name "Lennon" })
```

We can also make batch inserts using the insert-batch function. This function accepts the collection name followed by a sequence of maps representing the documents.

```
(monger.collection/insert-batch
  "users"
  [{ :first_name "John" :last_name "Doe" }
   { :first_name "Jane" :last_name "Smith" }])
```

Selecting Records

Monger provides several functions for searching for records and returning them as Clojure maps. These functions are find-maps, find-one-as-map, and find-map-by-id.

The find-maps function can query for documents in the collection using a map that contains the key and the value. Objects containing the key with the specified value are returned. All documents will be returned if no parameters are specified.

```
(monger.collection/find-maps "users" {:first_name "John"})
```

The find-one-as-map function will return a single object matching the query.

```
(monger.collection/find-one-as-map "users"
  { :first_name "John"})
```

Finally, the find-map-by-id function accepts an object ID as the search parameter.

```
(monger.collection/find-map-by-id "users"
  (ObjectId. "514f455d03642f52431b5bfe"))
```

It's also possible to use the standard MonogDB query operators in search queries, as seen here:

```
(monger.collection/find-maps "products" { :price { "$gt" 300 "$lte" 5000 } })
```

Updating Records

We update records by using the update function, which inserts the record if it doesn't exist when :upsert true is specified.

```
(update "users" { :first_name "John" :last_name "Doe" })
;;update existing or insert a new record
(update "users" { :first_name "John" :last_name "Doe" } :upsert true)
```

Deleting Records

Finally, we can delete documents from the database using the remove function. When no match criteria is specified, all documents are removed.

```
;;remove ALL documents
(monger.collection/remove "users")

;;remove documents with the specified key
(monger.collection/remove "users" { :language "English" })
```

As you can see, working with document-oriented databases is quite straightforward. Depending on your application needs, you may wish to use a document store instead of a relational store, or a combination of the two. Whatever approach you choose, Clojure has you covered.

Index

Clojure and Functional Patterns

Get up to speed on all that Clojure has to offer, and fine-tune your object thinking into a more functional style.

Programming Clojure (2nd edition)

If you want to keep up with the significant changes in this important language, you need the second edition of *Programming Clojure*. Stu and Aaron describe the modifications to the numerics system in Clojure 1.3, explain new Clojure concepts such as Protocols and Datatypes, and teach you how to think in Clojure.

Stuart Halloway and Aaron Bedra
(296 pages) ISBN: 9781934356869. $35
http://pragprog.com/book/shcloj2

Functional Programming Patterns in Scala and Clojure

Solve real-life programming problems with a fraction of the code that pure object-oriented programming requires. Use Scala and Clojure to solve in-depth problems and see how familiar object-oriented patterns can become more concise with functional programming and patterns. Your code will be more declarative, with fewer bugs and lower maintenance costs.

Michael Bevilacqua-Linn
(250 pages) ISBN: 9781937785475. $36
http://pragprog.com/book/mbfpp

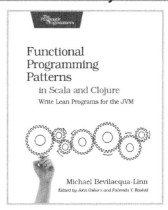

Long Live the Command Line!

Use tmux and Vim for incredible mouse-free productivity.

tmux

Your mouse is slowing you down. The time you spend
context switching between your editor and your con-
soles eats away at your productivity. Take control of
your environment with tmux, a terminal multiplexer
that you can tailor to your workflow. Learn how to
customize, script, and leverage tmux's unique abilities
and keep your fingers on your keyboard's home row.

Brian P. Hogan
(88 pages) ISBN: 9781934356968. $16.25
http://pragprog.com/book/bhtmux

Practical Vim

Vim is a fast and efficient text editor that will make
you a faster and more efficient developer. It's available
on almost every OS—if you master the techniques in
this book, you'll never need another text editor. In more
than 100 Vim tips, you'll quickly learn the editor's core
functionality and tackle your trickiest editing and
writing tasks.

Drew Neil
(346 pages) ISBN: 9781934356982. $29
http://pragprog.com/book/dnvim

The Joy of Math and Healthy Programming

Rediscover the joy and fascinating weirdness of pure mathematics, and learn how to take a healthier approach to programming.

Good Math

Mathematics is beautiful—and it can be fun and exciting as well as practical. *Good Math* is your guide to some of the most intriguing topics from two thousand years of mathematics: from Egyptian fractions to Turing machines; from the real meaning of numbers to proof trees, group symmetry, and mechanical computation. If you've ever wondered what lay beyond the proofs you struggled to complete in high school geometry, or what limits the capabilities of the computer on your desk, this is the book for you.

Mark C. Chu-Carroll
(282 pages) ISBN: 9781937785338. $34
http://pragprog.com/book/mcmath

The Healthy Programmer

To keep doing what you love, you need to maintain your own systems, not just the ones you write code for. Regular exercise and proper nutrition help you learn, remember, concentrate, and be creative—skills critical to doing your job well. Learn how to change your work habits, master exercises that make working at a computer more comfortable, and develop a plan to keep fit, healthy, and sharp for years to come.

This book is intended only as an informative guide for those wishing to know more about health issues. In no way is this book intended to replace, countermand, or conflict with the advice given to you by your own healthcare provider including Physician, Nurse Practitioner, Physician Assistant, Registered Dietician, and other licensed professionals.

Joe Kutner
(254 pages) ISBN: 9781937785314. $36
http://pragprog.com/book/jkthp

The Pragmatic Bookshelf

The Pragmatic Bookshelf features books written by developers for developers. The titles continue the well-known Pragmatic Programmer style and continue to garner awards and rave reviews. As development gets more and more difficult, the Pragmatic Programmers will be there with more titles and products to help you stay on top of your game.

Visit Us Online

This Book's Home Page
http://pragprog.com/book/dswdcloj
Source code from this book, errata, and other resources. Come give us feedback, too!

Register for Updates
http://pragprog.com/updates
Be notified when updates and new books become available.

Join the Community
http://pragprog.com/community
Read our weblogs, join our online discussions, participate in our mailing list, interact with our wiki, and benefit from the experience of other Pragmatic Programmers.

New and Noteworthy
http://pragprog.com/news
Check out the latest pragmatic developments, new titles and other offerings.

Save on the eBook

Save on the eBook versions of this title. Owning the paper version of this book entitles you to purchase the electronic versions at a terrific discount.

PDFs are great for carrying around on your laptop—they are hyperlinked, have color, and are fully searchable. Most titles are also available for the iPhone and iPod touch, Amazon Kindle, and other popular e-book readers.

Buy now at *http://pragprog.com/coupon*

Contact Us

Online Orders:	*http://pragprog.com/catalog*
Customer Service:	*support@pragprog.com*
International Rights:	*translations@pragprog.com*
Academic Use:	*academic@pragprog.com*
Write for Us:	*http://pragprog.com/write-for-us*
Or Call:	+1 800-699-7764

CPSIA information can be obtained at www.ICGtesting.com
Printed in the USA
LVOW03s1707020114

367790LV00004B/7/P